BUSINESS BASICS

CONDUCTING EFFECTIVE INTERVIEWS

How to find out what you need to know
and achieve the right results

Ann Dobson

I FEEL YOUR BODY LANGUAGE IS TRYING TO TELL US SOMETHING!

How To Books

Other books by the same author

How to Communicate at Work
How to Manage an Office
Managing Meetings
How to Write Business Letters
How to Return to Work

Cartoons by Mike Flanagan

British Library cataloguing-in-publication data
A catalogue record for this book is available from the British Library.

© Copyright 1996 by Ann Dobson.

First published in 1996 by How To Books Ltd, Plymbridge House,
Estover Road, Plymouth PL6 7PZ, United Kingdom.
Tel: (01752) 202301. Fax: (01752) 202331.

Note: The material contained in this book is set out in good faith for
general guidance and no liability can be accepted for loss or expense
incurred as a result of relying in particular circumstances on statements
made in the book. The laws and regulations are complex and liable to
change, and readers should check the current position with the relevant
authorities before making personal arrangements.

Produced for How To Books by Deer Park Productions.
Typeset by PDQ Typesetting, Stoke-on-Trent, Staffs.
Printed and bound by The Cromwell Press Ltd, Broughton Gifford,
Melksham, Wiltshire.

Contents

List of illustrations

Successful interviewing means much more than just asking questions and listening to the replies. For an interview to be a success a good deal of planning and preparation needs to be carried out beforehand.

Conducting Effective Interviews is aimed at both newcomers to interviewing and the more experienced interviewer. Part 1 offers a step by step guide to the general principles of interviewing and Part 2 gives more detailed information on the various types of interviews you may encounter in your working life. Throughout Part 2 case studies are used to show how the same interview can be dealt with in a successful or unsuccessful way.

At one time only senior management would carry out interviews. Nowadays, however, effective delegation in large organisations, coupled with the number of small businesses being set up, means that more and more working people at all levels are becoming involved in interviewing.

Whether you are interviewing a job applicant, dealing with disciplinary procedures or making someone redundant, *Conducting Effective Interviews* will provide you with all the information you need to enable you to achieve your aims.

Ann Dobson

IS THIS YOU?

Manager		Training Officer
	Supervisor	
Journalist		Counsellor
	Author	
Researcher		Solicitor
	Prison officer	
Personnel manager		Optician
	Police officer	
Practice manager		Lecturer
	Probation officer	
Driving instructor		Teacher
	Hotel manager	
Office manager		Publisher
	Social worker	
Financial adviser		Politician
	Employment consultant	
Sales manager		Retailer
	School governor	
Hospital administrator		Wholesaler
	Club chairperson	
Literary agent		Vet
	Doctor	
Building society manager		Accountant
	Bank manager	
Personal assistant		Surveyor
	Self employed	
Estate agent		Editor
	Insurance agent	
Dentist		Shopkeeper
	Mortgage broker	

1
Interviews in General

WHAT IS AN INTERVIEW?

An interview is a spoken **exchange of information**, usually between two people or between one person and a small group. This exchange of information involves speaking and listening on both sides. Usually, although not always, an interview is planned in advance.

An interview is different from an everyday 'chit chat' type of conversation, in that it should be structured and with a definite aim in mind.

WHY ARE INTERVIEWS SO IMPORTANT?

Interviews and meetings form an important part of the communication process in our modern society. Letters or telephone calls are another form of communication. But physical gestures cannot be registered whilst a telephone call takes place, and a letter can be written and re-written until it sounds exactly as the sender wishes. An interview, on the other hand, is instant, it is actually happening. At an interview an interaction of ideas takes place, true feelings can be expressed and both the interviewer and the interviewee should be able to achieve their objectives before the interview ends.

Different types of interview

There are many different types of interviews. These include:

- job selection interviews
- appraisal interviews
- promotion interviews
- coaching interviews
- counselling interviews
- grievance interviews

Becoming an effective interviewer

Are you finding:

- That interviews are a nightmare?

- That enthusiasm for interviews is a struggle?

- That it is hard to project the correct body language?

- That effective communication skills are a real problem?

- That the people you interview look bored and confused?

- That you would rather do anything other than conduct an interview?

If so, would you like to feel capable of:

- Being totally in control of every interview situation?

- Knowing exactly what you are going to say **before** the interview begins?

- Overcoming feelings of shyness and insecurity?

- Showing your own positive body language and reading the messages portrayed to you?

- Making other people feel at ease by the way you act towards them?

- Getting colleagues to do what you want?

- Putting across a really positive personal image?

- Improving the image of your organisation?

- Achieving the desired aims from your interview?

Have you said 'Yes'? Then read on!

Fig. 1. How conducting effective interviews can help *you*.

- disciplinary interviews
- dismissal interviews
- redundancy interviews
- student interviews.

Each of these will be discussed fully in Part 2. Suffice to say, however, that interviews in general form an important part of our everyday lives, and so long as they are effectively managed their results can be far-reaching and very beneficial to all concerned.

CONDUCTING ONE-TO-ONE INTERVIEWS

Most interviews are held on a one-to-one basis, *ie* one interviewer and one interviewee. Most of you have probably been interviewed yourself in the past, and so you know that it is very important for the interviewee to feel at ease and for the interviewer to establish a good rapport with them right from the start. If you feel nervous because you are a 'first time' interviewer, then consider how they will feel – far worse than you, no doubt!

In a one-to-one interview it is vital that you show your **control**. By all means start an interview with some friendly general questions, but do not allow the interview to become a social occasion. Move on to the main thrust of the interview as soon as possible, so that you do not waste valuable time on either side.

It is also vital to ensure that personal prejudices do not get in the way of your **judgement**. If you are, for instance, holding a job selection interview and a candidate walks in who reminds you of your ex-husband, whom you loathe, you must not allow your feelings to colour your attitude to this completely innocent stranger. Similarly, it is important not to take sides during, for instance, a grievance or counselling interview, but to look at all the facts and take an unbiased decision on what should be done.

HOLDING GROUP INTERVIEWS

When we talk about group interviews we mean one interviewee and several interviewers. Other types of group discussion would be more properly called meetings rather than interviews. Group interviews usually apply to job selection, and the group is often known as a 'panel'. Sometimes one member of the panel is in charge, which is often a good idea so that the interviewee knows who to address for at least most of the time.

There are advantages and disadvantages to group interviews:

Advantages

- Each member of the group will normally have a specific role to play according to their own specialist knowledge.

- There is less likelihood of biases resulting from individual 'gut' feelings (although this should not happen in a well conducted interview anyway).

- The responsibility for the interview will usually be shared equally between the group.

Disadvantages

- The interviewee might feel so nervous that he or she cannot participate effectively at the interview.

- Reaching a final decision on the right person for the job might be difficult if the group members disagree.

- Members of the group may feel uncomfortable with one another, thus creating a strained environment for everyone.

CHOOSING FORMALITY OR INFORMALITY: QUESTIONS AND ANSWERS

What do we think of as a formal interview?
An interview that has been properly planned and arranged in advance.

But are all pre-arranged interviews formal occasions?
No, they are not. An interview can be arranged months in advance and still be an informal occasion.

So how about a dismissal interview for gross misconduct, carried out immediately the decision to dismiss a member of staff was taken. Would that be a formal interview?
Yes, it would, because of the very nature of the interview.

The above questions and answers illustrate the overlap between formal and informal interviews. It has to be said, however, that the vast majority will be formal in the sense that they will be pre-arranged and prepared for, with or without written notes being taken during or after the interview takes place. Even so-called formal interviews do not have to be stuffy, though. They can still, in most cases, be a lively interchange of information and ideas.

There is a danger that informal interviews can easily turn into a chat, with little being achieved as a result. The only real exception to this is when informal interviews are being held as a first stage in job selection. This usually involves inviting several prospective candidates along for coffee and an informal talk before showing them around the organisation. This gives the candidates a chance to get the feel of the place and the prospective employer a chance to decide who might be suitable for more formal interviewing at a later stage.

CHECKLIST

- Do you know the purpose of an interview?

- Are you aware of why interviews are so important?

- Do you know the advantages and disadvantages of group interviews?

- Do you feel confident with one-to-one interviews?

- Are most of your interviews formal in nature?

- If so, do you still manage to make them enjoyable for both parties?

- Are you aware of the value of informal interviews for the first stage in job selection?

DISCUSSION POINTS

1. What would you see as the essential skills for an effective interviewer?

2. Do you think that interviews, like meetings, can be a waste of time and effort?

3. What are your views on group interviews as a way of job selection?

2
Planning and Research

GATHERING INFORMATION

The amount of information needed for an interview varies according to the type of interview involved. For instance, for a job selection interview the interviewer will need a copy of the applicant's **CV** and any correspondence, together with the **job description** and, if appropriate, the **job specification** (see Chapter 6). Similarly, before a disciplinary interview takes place, the person's **personnel file** should be to hand, as well as any **written warnings** that might have been issued prior to interview. It may also be necessary to obtain information from other members of staff who have been involved with the person being disciplined.

When all the relevant information is to hand, it is important that you spare some time to read through the paperwork, making notes of the main points you want to raise at interview.

Advance preparation for an interview, in the form of background information, will always pay off. If you know what you are talking about and what you want to achieve from the interview before you begin, then your objectives are far more likely to have been achieved by the time the interview ends.

DECIDING ON THE LOCATION

An interview can be held almost anywhere. In reality, however, most interviews are held in a business connection and therefore tend to take place in an office environment. Occasionally, however, they will be held at a hotel or other public place.

Advantages of an office environment
- Familiarity for yourself, giving you more confidence to conduct the interview.

- Ease of planning and preparation if the interview is to be held in the same building.

- More of an 'official' feel to an interview held in an office.

Disadvantages of an office environment

- More formality for the interviewee, who might feel intimidated.

- Neutral ground, such as a hotel, is sometimes better for private interviews.

- An open plan office can be unsuitable for an interview – see below.

Coping with an open plan office
It is particularly important to be aware of the problems of conducting interviews in an open plan office environment. Open plan offices are generally very noisy and lacking in privacy. They can inhibit your interviewee and may well result in a completely ineffective interview. Of course, there are exceptions and some open plan offices are designed with peace and privacy in mind, but they are definitely in the minority. If you work in an open plan office it might be a good idea to book a room somewhere else in the building for your interview, particularly if the subject of the interview is confidential or controversial.

When an interview is taking place at a hotel or leisure club, a drink beforehand, or even a quick swim in the indoor leisure pool, can get the proceedings off to a very promising start, but obviously only in certain circumstances. Taking part in a companionable swim with a colleague you are about to promote is one thing, but would not be so appealing if you are about to fire the person in question!

It is very important to ensure that wherever the meeting takes place you have **no interruptions** either in person or on the telephone during the proceedings. A telephone that rings constantly is not conducive to a free-flowing interview situation. You might not mind, particularly if the call is one you were waiting for, but your interviewee will probably lose his or her train of thought and begin to feel that you value your telephone conversation more highly than the interview taking place.

NOTIFYING THE INTERVIEWEES

It is very easy to plan and prepare for an interview and forget one

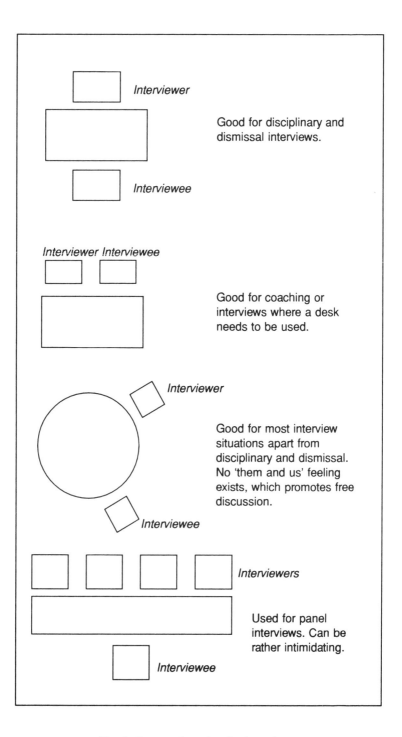

Fig. 2. Suggested seating for interviews.

vital ingredient – the person or persons who are to attend. Make sure you notify everyone involved well in advance, otherwise you might just be sitting at the interview all on your own.

Written notification is always better than a telephone call, whenever time permits. Telephone calls can be forgotten with the pressure of other business, whereas a brief letter, stating the day, time, place and purpose of the interview is the best method of ensuring attendance.

Remember that the person you are interviewing might need time to prepare for the interview, just the same as you. For example, with an appraisal interview, the interviewee will probably want to ask you just as many questions as you intend to ask them. They will not be in a position to do this unless they can get their thoughts organised before the interview takes place.

ARRANGING THE ROOM

The way that a room is arranged for an interview can have an important bearing on the outcome. A dark-walled, dingy office with no character, no pictures, no window and nothing to inspire anyone in any way will do little to enhance your interviewing skills. Neither will a room with too many distractions, such as an outstanding collection of porcelain china in a glass cabinet, or a series of pictures all around the walls.

In between these two extremes lies the perfect interview room. It should be pleasantly decorated and furnished, with a few pictures and human touches scattered about in a natural fashion. The overall effect should be one of **efficiency** and **practicality**, coupled with a feeling of comfort and well-being.

Positioning the furniture

Suggested furniture layouts are shown in Figure 2. With the possible exception of a dismissal interview, it is usually better not to sit behind a desk. This can intimidate the interviewee, and create a 'them and us' confrontation. Instead you could:

- sit in front or at the side of your desk, so that you can still use it without seeming to put up a barrier

- arrange some easy chairs around a circular coffee table and sit there with your interviewee

- go one step further and organise comfy sofas and lots of refreshments to entice your interviewees into the 'feel' of the interview (this, of course, would only be suitable for a pleasant interview situation).

STRUCTURING THE INTERVIEW: QUESTIONS AND ANSWERS

What is the purpose of your interview?
(Give your own answer.)

How long will the interview last?
(Give your own answer.)

What do you hope to achieve?
(Give your own answer.)

Can you answer the questions above? You should be able to, because it is vitally important for your purpose and objectives to be clear to both you and your interviewee. If you have no clearly planned structure, then your interview will fail.

Every interview, just the same as every meeting or every business letter, should have:

- a beginning
- a middle
- an end.

The beginning
The beginning of the interview will include welcoming the interviewee and making them feel at ease, usually by exchanging a few pleasantries before coming on to the matter in hand.

The middle
This is the main thrust of the interview. Have a list of everything you intend to cover and make sure you keep to that list. Keep to your allocated time limit too. No one has time to waste on irrelevances. In the business world of today time is money.

The end
This is when you should summarise, both for yourself and your interviewee, the main points of the interview. Make sure you are both clear about what is to happen next before you bring the interview to its conclusion.

Always remember that a well structured interview is a successful interview. Once again, this comes back to planning and preparation beforehand. After all, an actor cannot perform well on the London stage unless he has learned his lines first. As an interviewer you do not need to learn your lines but you do still have to give a considerable amount of thought and preparation to the interview about to take place.

CHECKLIST

● Have you gathered together all the relevant information?

● Have you spent sufficient time reading this information?

● Have you decided on the location for your interview?

● Have you notified the interviewee/s?

● Have you arranged the room in a way that is appropriate for the type of interview?

● Have you given thought to the structuring of your interview?

● Have you fixed a time limit for the interview?

● Have you decided exactly what you want to achieve from the interview?

DISCUSSION POINTS

1. How much influence do you think the location has on the success of an interview? Do you think that perhaps the room layout is more important?

2. 'Adequate planning and preparation form the basis of a successful interview.' Discuss this statement.

3. Do you think every interview should have a time limit? If not, when do you think it would be appropriate to leave the timing open?

3
Speaking and Listening Skills

GIVING THE RIGHT IMPRESSION

Whatever type of interview you are conducting it is very important for you to give the right impression. This impression will, of course, vary according to the situation. For instance, opening with 'I'm really pleased that you could come and see us today' would be fine for a job interview, but hardly appropriate for a dismissal interview.

When unpleasant interviews are necessary, always try to act like a human being with real feelings. A superior or patronising approach will not achieve the desired objectives. Under no circumstances should you be rude either. You have to maintain a reputation as a fair-minded person, and making enemies will get you nowhere.

Your appearance

You may be thinking that appearance does not come into speaking and listening skills and to an extent you would be right, but it is important to **dress correctly** in order to give support to what you say. For instance, if you interview applicants for a job whilst you are in scruffy clothes and badly in need of a bath, you cannot expect the applicant to want to work for you anyway or for anything you say to be taken seriously.

Remember above all that you are on show at the interview and will be judged by the interviewee/s in exactly the same way as you will be judging them. Give thought and effort to ensuring that you project the right image at all times, so that you are then in a position to demand high standards of others.

Question and answer
How can I be sure that I am giving the right impression when interviewing?
You can never be sure, but so long as you have dressed carefully, prepared well, and acted in a way that is natural to you then you

have done your best to give the right impression.

USING APPROPRIATE WORDS

Did you have a teacher at school who, brilliant though he or she may have been, just could not teach a class?
If you have answered 'yes', then that person was failing to communicate in a way that you could understand.

Unfortunately, this lack of communication does not apply just to a teacher/pupil situation. In all walks of life we have to use the right words to be understood.

During the course of an interview you need to express your ideas, thoughts and feelings in an easy to understand manner, so that the person being interviewed understands exactly what you are trying to say. Do not try to impress by using long and complicated words. All these will do is cause confusion. Behave in a normal way. Speak as you would normally speak and behave in a way that feels comfortable to you.

Managing your voice
The way we use our voice is almost as important as what we say. Take care that you do not do any of the following:

- Speak in a high pitched whining voice which is very hard on the ears.

- Speak so softly that no one else can hear without straining.

- Speak in a grating voice, also very hard on the ears.

- Speak so fast that you are difficult to understand.

- Use phrases repeatedly, such as 'Right', 'You know', 'Know what I mean?' and the very trendy and perhaps most irritating of all: 'Cool' as an answer to statements made to you!

Above all, just **be yourself** and make sure that everything you say is both accurate in content and relevant to the interview. Never quote something that could be challenged: for example, 'We offer the very best rates in the area'. The person you are interviewing might just know somewhere offering better rates, and you will then be made to look insincere and unsure of your facts.

ASKING QUESTIONS

Questions obviously form a very important part of any interview. You will need to ask your interviewee questions and they will normally have prepared questions to ask you.

There are two main types of questions – open and closed.

Open questions

An example of an open question is: 'Tell me why you would like to work here.' This type of question requires a detailed answer.

Advantages
- A good deal of information can be gained.

- They can put the interviewee at ease.

- The same questions can be put to different interviewees, *eg* at a job selection interview, and the answers compared.

Disadvantages
- They can encourage the interviewee to 'waffle'.

- They can lead to exceeding the time limit for the interview.

- They can be misunderstood unless carefully phrased.

Closed questions

An example of a closed question is: 'How long have you been with us now, James?' This type of question requires a direct and short answer.

Advantages
- They extract a simple answer quickly.

- They take up a minimum amount of time.

- They can keep an interview moving at a brisk pace.

Disadvantages
- Only a limited amount of information can be gained.

- The interview can sound rather like 'twenty questions' if too many closed questions are used in close succession.

- Because only one or a few words are necessary, it is easier to lie or bluff.

Whenever you have a particularly awkward question to ask be very careful how you phrase it. The required answer should be obtained with the minimum embarrassment either to you or the other person.

Tips to help you ask your questions

- Make a list beforehand of the questions to be asked.

- Ask one question at a time. Asking lots of questions at once will cause confusion and won't produce good answers.

- Wait for an answer to your question before moving on to the next one.

- Listen carefully to the answer so that you really understand it.

- If the answer does not satisfy you, ask another question. Always remember, however, that questions should be asked for specific reasons, not just as a way of interrupting.

- Try to alternate your open and closed questions to introduce an element of surprise and originality into the interview.

LISTENING TO OTHERS

Question: How do you find out the most about other people?

- By asking questions?
- By listening?

Answer: Both. We must first of all ask the right questions and then listen carefully when we are given the answers.

Good listeners are very hard to find. Listening, unlike speaking, is not taught to us as children. It is something we have to pick up as we go along. It is an art, and many of us are far too busy getting on with our own lives to listen properly to what others have to say.

In an interview situation particularly listening is very important.

From it we can learn a great deal of valuable information. We spend as much time listening as speaking in our everyday working life. The problem is that a lot of what we listen to we do not retain and then what we hear is no use to us at all.

Tips to help you become a good listener

- Look interested in what is being said. It might not sound riveting but the information you are receiving will probably be needed later on.

- Take notes if necessary, so that what you hear is retained.

- Do not interrupt whilst the interviewee is speaking.

- Help the other person along by giving the occasional nod or smile.

- Do not pre-judge. Give the interviewee a chance even if you are sure that you will not agree with his or her views.

- Try not to let your mind wander. Admittedly, the coming weekend might be more exciting to think about, but you must do your best to keep your mind on the job!

SUMMARISING THE OUTCOME

It is quite a good idea as the interview progresses to summarise all the key points, so that both parties are fully aware of what is being discussed and decided upon. Then, at the end of the interview you can sum up once again, this time taking the interview as a whole and stating the outcome as you see it. Make sure that your interviewee agrees with your interpretation of what has gone on.

The extent to which summarising is necessary will, of course, vary according to the type of interview taking place. It is not really relevant to pay much attention to summarising with a job selection interview, but it could be extremely relevant at an appraisal or disciplinary interview.

With every type of interview, it is very important for you to make a few notes yourself either during or after the interview. Unless the meeting is a very formal occasion, such as a disciplinary, redundancy or dismissal interview, these can just be rough notes for you to refer to later.

CHECKLIST

- Do you give the right impression when interviewing?

- If not, how do you think you can improve things?

- Are the words you use easy to understand?

- Do you give thought to the pitch and clarity of your speech?

- Do you use a good mixture of open and closed questions at your interviews?

- Do you take the time out to listen carefully to the answers you are given?

- Can you effectively summarise the main points of an interview, both for your benefit and for the benefit of the person you are interviewing?

DISCUSSION POINTS

1. If you were recruiting for a secretarial position, would the clothes worn by the interviewees affect your judgement of their ability to do the job?

2. 'Show your superiority. Show them who's boss.' How true do you think this statement is when applied to job selection interviewing?

3. Do you think you use enough open questions in your interviews? If not, why do you think this is?

4
Using and Interpreting Body Language

UNDERSTANDING BODY LANGUAGE

Body language, sometimes known as non-verbal communication, refers to the way we communicate by using different parts of our body. The messages we convey can be deliberate, such as a smile or a frown, or they can be involuntary such as a shiver. Body language is often said to be the way we show the emotional side of our relationships, and its effective use can tell us far more than any words that accompany it.

Body language is a very complicated subject and we only touch on the basics here. There are people, particularly those in the media, whose body language is the key to their success and they have to work on their image constantly. For most of us, however, body language makes up just part of our day-to-day dealings with other people, but the more attention we pay to it, the more successful our business and personal relationships are likely to be.

MAKING BODY LANGUAGE WORK FOR YOU

In an interview it is important that your body language is interpreted in the way you want it to be, and honesty is not always the best policy. You could have the unenviable task of interviewing a member of your staff with a view to dismissal, and you might totally despise the person sitting in front of you, but you must not let your true feelings show. After all, you are there to do a job and it is up to you to make sure that your interview fulfils its objectives.

Always remember too that the person being interviewed could be very nervous and an encouraging smile or a nod occasionally will be well received, whatever the purpose of the interview.

Each type of interview requires different body language. At a disciplinary interview, looking the person piercingly in the eye as you question them may be the best way of getting to the truth, whilst a sympathetic, caring approach will encourage a nervous person at a counselling interview.

With practice you can make your body language work in exactly the way you want it to. It is then equally important to ensure that what you say supports your body language.

READING OTHER PEOPLE'S BODY LANGUAGE

We can learn a lot by watching other people and interpreting their body language. Next time you travel on a bus or a train, study the people travelling with you. Try to imagine what they are really like, what their job is, where they live and what problems they have in their business or personal life. You are not being nosy, you are just interpreting their body language, and it can be a fascinating hobby if you have sufficient time to devote to it.

Revealing body language

At your interviews always watch carefully for revealing body language. The particular points to look for are:

Eye contact
People who look at you are likely to be listening carefully to what you are saying. Those who look away whenever you talk to them are either nervous or have something to hide.

Body direction
At the beginning of an interview, the interviewee will normally be facing you. If, as the interview progresses, they begin to turn away, that suggests they are no longer interested in what you are saying.

Posture
If your interviewee is paying attention then he or she is likely to be sitting slightly forward in the seat, ready to contribute at the appropriate time. On the other hand, slouching back in a chair suggests lack of interest and even boredom.

Head movements
Look for positive or negative head movements. Most of us nod or shake our head in agreement or disagreement almost unconsciously and you will learn a lot from other people if you watch for these natural reactions to what you are saying.

Basically, if you get a blank, bored expression, which changes very little no matter what you say or do, then your interviewing skills could perhaps do with a bit more polishing. Always remember that, with few exceptions, an interview should be an exhilarating, positive exchange of information and ideas, not a boring session that both parties cannot wait to end.

WATCHING OUT FOR IRRITATING HABITS

We all have irritating habits. After all, none of us is perfect. When you are interviewing someone, however, try very hard to keep your habits under control. For instance, it is really very irritating for someone to watch you repeatedly scratch your head, bite your nails, drum your fingers on the table, or fiddle with a pencil whilst they are trying to respond to what you are saying to them. Make sure that you keep yourself well in check, and that you have not slipped into an irritating habit without even realising it.

DEALING WITH AN ATTITUDE PROBLEM

You have probably heard the expression, 'Oh, he/she has an attitude problem'. What exactly do we mean? The dictionary defines 'attitude' as 'a way of thinking and behaving'. An attitude problem therefore means that the person in question thinks and behaves in a manner that is unacceptable to others.

Perhaps you have interviewed people with an attitude problem, but has it ever occurred to you that you might just have one too? An interviewer with an attitude problem is unlikely to gain the respect of the people he or she interviews, so why not check your attitude for yourself?

Questions
1. Do you resent being told what to do?
2. Do you resent being told how to do something, even if you don't know how to do it yourself?
3. Do you resent authority in any shape or form?
4. Do you turn up late for your interviews, inappropriately dressed, and then proceed to treat your interviewees as second-class citizens?
5. Did you dislike being told what to do at school?

Answers
A 'yes' answer to most of these questions means you probably do

have an attitude problem that other people will have noticed by watching your body language as well as by listening to what you have to say.

Sort out your attitude problem by trying the following:

- Identify the reason why you feel the need to 'kick' against everyone. This might go back to your childhood. Perhaps you had an unstable background or had to compete with very clever brothers or sisters.

- Ask yourself what you are gaining from your actions.

- Assuming you decide that you are gaining nothing, make up your mind that it is time for a change.

- Work on the 'new you' next time you interview someone.

- Afterwards, assess the results. Hopefully your interview will have been much more successful than previously.

Even the slightest degree of an attitude problem needs prompt treatment, so that you become a more respected and better liked person. Although to a certain extent you hold the upper hand in an interview situation, the person you are interviewing should never be made to feel inferior or undermined in any way. The secret of a successful interview is making the other person feel that they are being listened to and treated fairly. If you show an arrogant attitude, they will respond accordingly, and the effectiveness of the interview will be lost.

CHECKLIST

- Do you understand what body language is?

- Are you aware of how important it can be at interviews?

- Can you use the correct body language for the occasion?

- Are you able to interpret other people's body language correctly?

- Do you have any irritating habits?

- Have you got an attitude problem?

- If so, what do you intend to do about it?

1. Greet the person on arrival.

2. Offer a seat and wait for the other person to sit down.

3. Smile encouragingly as you begin the interview.

4. Look the person in the eye as you speak.

5. Sit up straight and look alert and confident.

6. Speak in a controlled manner, varying the tone of your voice.

7. Nod and shake your head to show interest in what is being said to you.

8. Use hand gestures to emphasise various points.

9. Make sure that your body language says what you want it to say at all times.

10. Shake hands at the end of the interview and show the person out of the room.

Fig. 3. Ten steps to effective body language.

DISCUSSION POINTS

1. 'Body language tells us more than words can ever say.' Discuss this statement and say why you think it is true or false.

2. In what ways do you think you can show positive body language to a person who comes to you for a counselling interview?

3. Watch a friend or a business colleague for a few minutes. See if they have any visible irritating habits and if so write them down. Then think about yourself and write down your own deficiencies. If you know the person well enough you can compare notes!

5
Job Selection Interviews

Face-to-face interviews are the most popular way of recruiting staff, and yet unless they are organised and conducted in an effective manner, what they tell us about a person's suitability for the job is negligible.

A positive job selection interview is one where the interviewer knows the 'blueprint' of the person he or she is looking for and spends the entire interview assessing whether the applicant seated in the chair fills that requirement. Few compromises should be necessary. Someone, somewhere must be able to fit the bill, particularly in today's competitive job market.

It is very important that you liaise, at each stage of the proceedings, with any other members of staff who will be involved with the person to be appointed.

DOING THE GROUNDWORK

Writing a job description

A job description, as its name implies, describes the job on offer. This makes it clear to both you and the job applicant what is required of them. The job description is generally sent out in advance of the interview.

If an accurate job description is prepared, apart from being useful at the interview, it will also serve as a reminder to both of you in the future. For instance, if you try adding on extra responsibilities, your employee can retaliate by saying 'I'm not doing that because it is not my job'. You will then be able to check the job description to see who is right. It should be mentioned, however, that many employers get round the problem of a job description being 'law' by adding a sentence at the bottom saying something like, 'These duties may be amended from time to time at the discretion of the management'. A typical job description is shown in Figure 4.

ROSE LANE CARAVAN SITE

Job description

Job title: Receptionist

Responsible to: Site Manager

Place of work: Rose Lane Caravan Site

Salary scale: £8,000 pa

Days of work: Shift system in operation to include weekends

Hours of work: Week 1 – 0830 hrs – 1730 hrs Monday–Friday
                      Week 2 – 1300 hrs – 1730 hrs Monday–Friday
                      plus 0830 hrs – 1300 hrs Saturday and Sunday

Holidays: 4 weeks per annum plus public holidays

Duties and responsibilities:

1.   Speaking to members of the public both on the telephone
      and in person.

2.   Dealing with bookings for both caravans and tents.

3.   Undertaking the typing of letters, memos and reports and
      generally helping the office manager.

4.   Assisting the bar manager when he needs secretarial
      support.

These duties may be amended from time to time at the
discretion of the Site Manager.

                                              January 19XX

Fig. 4. A typical job description.

```
┌─────────────────────────────────────────────────────────┐
│                                                           │
│                ROSE LANE CARAVAN SITE                     │
│                                                           │
│                                                           │
│                   Job specification                       │
│                                                           │
│                                                           │
│   Job title:              Receptionist                    │
│                                                           │
│                                                           │
│   Responsible to:         Site Manager                    │
│                                                           │
│                                                           │
│   Place of work:          Rose Lane Caravan Site          │
│                                                           │
│                                                           │
│   Age range:              18–30 years                     │
│                                                           │
│                                                           │
│   Educational background  Educated to GCSE standard (or   │
│   and qualifications:     equivalent) in English, Maths,  │
│                           and three other subjects, all   │
│                           in Grade C or above.            │
│                                                           │
│                           RSA Stage III or Pitman         │
│                           Advanced Typewriting.           │
│                                                           │
│                           RSA Stage II or Pitman          │
│                           Intermediate Word Processing.   │
│                                                           │
│                                                           │
│   Skills and personal     Smart, well groomed appearance. │
│   qualities required:     Ability to mix well and work on │
│                           own initiative.                 │
│                                                           │
│                                                           │
│   Previous work           Experience in an office an      │
│   experience:             advantage but not essential.    │
│                                                           │
│                                                           │
│   Health record:          Should be in good general       │
│                           health.                         │
│                                                           │
└─────────────────────────────────────────────────────────┘
```

Fig. 5. A typical job specification.

Interview schedule for receptionist vacancy

Monday 12 February 19XX

0900 hrs Sharon Wallace – aged 20

0930 hrs Rosemary Fisher – aged 29

1000 hrs Paula White – aged 24

1030 hrs Coffee

1100 hrs Susan Sharpe – aged 19

1130 hrs Rachel Minster aged 25

1200 hrs Anna Smith – aged 20

1230 hrs Sarah Clark – aged 28

1300 hrs Lunch

1400 hrs Anne Edwards – aged 21

1430 hrs Charlotte West – aged 18

1500 hrs Caroline Sumner – aged 20

Fig. 6. Example interview schedule.

Deciding on the job specification

Whereas the **job description** identifies the nature of the job on offer, the **job specification** identifies the type of employee required to fill that job. The job specification should always be produced after the job description.

The job specification is particularly important at the interview. Check carefully to see how many criteria each applicant fulfils, and keep to the standards you have set. It is no use conveniently forgetting, for instance, that an applicant you like has no computer experience, if your job specification specifically states that the job demands someone who is computer literate. A typical job specification is shown in Figure 5.

Drawing up a shortlist

It is largely up to you or your organisation to decide how you want people to apply for the job you are offering. The most usual way is to ask them to send in a **written letter** and a **curriculum vitae** (CV). Some organisations ask for an application form to be filled in too, because this is more standard than a CV for comparison purposes. It is also a good idea to state a **closing date** when you advertise, so that you know when you can start sifting through the applications to arrive at a shortlist for interview.

Selecting the candidates
Firstly, decide how many applicants you wish to interview. Next, keeping your job description and job specification in front of you, go through the applications and make a pile of 'definites', a pile of 'possibles' and a pile of 'definitely nots'. The latter category can be discarded immediately, but it is common courtesy to send a short letter explaining that their application was not successful. See how many 'definites' you have and, if necessary, make up the required number by adding a few 'possibles'. Write to the remaining 'possibles' in the same way as the 'definitely nots'.

Choosing the interview days
Work out the day or days you will be available to hold the interviews and work out a proper schedule. Allow a set amount of time for each person and make sure you give yourself ample tea/coffee/lunch breaks. Do not be over-ambitious in the number of applicants you fit into one day. It is your duty to give everyone your best attention and you cannot do that if you are exhausted at the end of interviewing say 25 applicants in a single day. A sample interview schedule is shown in Figure 6.

Notifying the chosen applicants
Finally, send a letter to those applicants who have been selected for interview. This letter should be sent out approximately a fortnight beforehand, so that if anyone cannot attend on the day given they will have plenty of time to let you know.

CONDUCTING THE INTERVIEW

Welcoming each applicant
First impressions count for a lot – on both sides. You may well have positive or negative thoughts every time someone walks in to be interviewed, but how about them? How you greet every applicant will have a strong bearing on their performance during the interview.

Almost without exception, everyone feels nervous when they attend a job interview, and it is up to you to put them at ease. Begin by opening your door and welcoming the applicant personally, smiling reassuringly as you show them a comfortable seat, preferably close to yours. Start the interview by talking about the weather, their journey, the picture on the wall, in fact anything other than the purpose of the interview.

As soon as you feel you have put the other person at ease, you can then explain the purpose of the interview and how you intend to conduct the proceedings.

Establishing a rapport
In order to establish a good rapport with the applicant it is important for you to explain everything necessary about the job on offer. Give them as many details as you can about both the job and the organisation you represent, so that they can start to build up a picture of what they would be doing, where they would be working and with whom they would be mixing.

Your over-riding aim should be to show that you are human, with feelings and failings just the same as anyone else. The applicant sitting with you will probably feel inferior and unimportant and your job is to eliminate these feelings so that you get to know the 'real' person behind the apprehensive façade.

Do not rush an interview, even if it means you run a little late. Some applicants will deal with questions more quickly than others. After all we are all individuals and your interviews would become pretty boring affairs if everyone answered questions in exactly the same way and in exactly the same amount of time.

Asking the right questions

The questions you ask should give you the information you need to know, and these can be planned well in advance. As we have said before, there are two types of questions:

- **Open ended** where the applicant is encouraged to speak at length, rather than answer with one or just a few words – *eg* 'Why would you like to work for us?'

- **Closed** where a short answer will suffice – *eg* 'How many years have you worked at Farmers?'

The following are standard questions that should be asked at almost all job selection interviews. There is no one 'correct' answer to any of them. By using your job description, job specification and the candidate's CV/application, you should know what answers you require for your own individual purposes.

Their job
- Tell me about the tasks and responsibilities involved in your present/most recent job.

- Describe a day at work.

- How well do you mix with your work colleagues?

The job on offer
- What interests you about this job?

- Are you prepared to work late if and when necessary?

- Why do you think you would be suitable for this position?

- Are you looking for a long-term commitment?

- Will you be interested in promotion?

Personal traits
- Tell me about yourself.

- Do you consider yourself to be a popular person?

- What do you see as your strengths and weaknesses?

- Can you work in a team?

- Are you any good at making decisions?

- Can you cope in a crisis?

There will obviously be other, more specific, questions you may want to ask, relating to the particular position being filled, but the above, if answered fully, will give you a good indication of who you are dealing with.

At some job interviews 'role play' is included, where you pretend, for instance, that you are an irate visitor to the reception desk and the interviewee is given the opportunity to deal with this situation.

Listening and assessing

Whilst your questions are being answered listen very carefully and watch the applicant's body language. If they look you fully in the eye, then they are likely to be telling the truth. If they look at their feet all the time, they are either extremely shy or nervous, or else they are hiding something from you. You must try to get to the truth and really penetrate any outer barrier that might have been consciously or unconsciously put up.

In an effective interview situation the applicant should be speaking for around three quarters of the time and you for just one quarter. Make notes so that you can refer to them later, and try to assess the character and abilities of the person you are listening to. Don't forget that you want to see the 'real' person, not someone who is very good at play acting.

FOLLOWING UP

Organising second interviews

Second interviews are not always necessary. If someone suitable can be selected the first time then that is obviously best from both points of view, but sometimes it can be difficult deciding just who to appoint.

A first interview deals with the facts and the basic ability of the applicant. A second interview is usually more 'in depth'. You will already know the person (assuming you conducted the first interview), so you can concentrate on their suitability for the job.

Giving thought to character

The second interview also offers an opportunity to look a little closer at the applicant's character. How do they come across to you? Have they got too much to say for themselves, or too little? Are they cocky? Do they have an 'attitude problem'? Look carefully: once you have given them the job it is too late to do anything other than put up with what could prove to be very irritating characteristics.

Making the right decision

There is only so much you can do to ensure you have picked the right person for the job. Sooner or later a decision will need to be made on who to select. Make sure that your decision is taken without any prejudice on your part. Everyone should be judged equally regardless of their sex, colour or religion. Theoretically age should be disregarded too, but there are sometimes grounds for taking age into consideration with certain types of jobs obviously more suited to either the younger or more mature applicant.

In the unlikely event that after the second interviews have been held you still feel there is no one suitable for the job then don't settle for second best. You will just have to re-advertise the vacancy and start the process all over again.

Contacting the successful applicant

Assuming you do make a decision and decide to appoint someone, that person should be notified **as soon as possible**. You can do this by telephone initially, but then you should send a written letter confirming all the details. Often enclosed with such a letter is the **contract of employment** which clearly sets out what is expected of the new employee and what they can expect in return. It is very important to get this contract right as it can form the basis of any disciplinary proceedings, should they ever be necessary.

Notifying the other applicants

Once the job offer has been accepted you should write to the unsuccessful applicants explaining to them that the vacancy has been filled. Remember to thank them for attending for interview and you can, if you wish, say that you will keep their application on file in case a vacancy should arise in the future.

QUESTIONS AND ANSWERS

How do I know I have chosen the right person for the job?

You never know for certain until that person has proved him/herself one way or the other. You can only do your best, by asking the correct questions and carefully analysing the answers you are given.

If someone I interview seems immediately suitable can I offer them the job before I have seen everyone else?
You can, but you would be foolish to do so. After all, you might think this person is very suitable, but someone attending later could be 100 per cent perfect and then you will regret having been so hasty. Make absolutely sure before offering anything to anyone.

I feel awful having to write to unsuccessful job applicants. Is there a kind way of doing this?
Say in your letter that the response to the advertisement was overwhelming and that you have had a difficult choice compiling a shortlist/choosing an applicant. Thank the person for applying and say that, although they have not been chosen this time, you would be pleased to hear from them should another vacancy arise in the future. Above all, don't make them feel a failure. Let them think that sheer weight of numbers has stopped them being successful this time.

CHECKLIST

Before
- Have you decided on the job description and job specification?

- Have you advertised the vacancy?

- Have you sifted through the CVs and applications in order to draw up a shortlist?

- Have you prepared a realistic interview schedule?

During
- Have you welcomed the applicant?

- Have you established a rapport and made the person feel at ease?

- Have you outlined the details of the job on offer?

- Have you asked the right questions?

- Have you listened to the answers?

After
- Have you organised second interviews?

- Have you given thought to the applicant's character?

- Have you made the right decision?

- Have you notified the successful applicant?

- Have you followed up a verbal conformation with a written letter and a contract of employment?

- Have you also notified the unsuccessful applicants?

CASE STUDIES

Introduction
Throughout this section, ten case studies are used to show a cross-section of the different types of people involved in interviewing and the various interview situations they may find themselves in.

James Rowe, Customer Liaison Manager
James, aged 40, works for a large, newly privatised, passenger airline. His job includes promoting the airline as well as dealing with complaints from the general public. He is responsible for the hiring and firing of his own departmental staff.

Anna Jones, Head of Business Studies Department
Anna, aged 35, has recently been promoted to this position, in a college of further education. She is responsible for interviewing both staff and students.

Sonia, Practice Manager
Sonia, aged 30, works for a busy health centre where she is responsible, amongst other things, for the recruitment and welfare of all the non-medical staff.

Alex, Personnel Manager
Alex, aged 50, works for one of the privatised water companies. He is a very busy man, having to divide his time equally between appointing staff and organising on-going staff assessment programmes.

Sarah, Social Worker
Sarah, aged 45, works in a local geriatric hospital. She is responsible for organising follow-up care for patients who are leaving the hospital. This often involves interviewing the patients themselves, and/or their relatives. As senior social worker for the group she also helps the new social workers who come on to their team.

John, Sales Manager
John, aged 38, works for a large garage group. He has just been promoted from senior sales rep to sales manager and has never been involved in interviewing before.

Nicky, Catering Company Owner
Nicky, aged 20, already has her own catering company and is a definite high flyer. Her parents have backed her financially and although the company has only been going for a year, it is already very successful. Nicky employs 15 staff and runs her business from a small shop in her home town.

Phil, Station Officer
Phil, aged 40, works for the Fire Service. He is in charge of his own 'watch' and deals with all the day-to-day running of the team.

Martin, Driving Instructor
Martin, aged 46, has just set up his own driving school. He was made redundant by the post office after 25 years' service, and this is a completely new venture for him.

Phillip, Department Store Owner
Phillip is only 32, but his department store has been in the family for generations. It is situated in a busy town and has a reputation built up over so many years that business is always booming. The store is on three floors and has 20 different departments. Phillip insists on taking all personnel matters on his own shoulders as he thinks, like his father before him, that the store's main asset is its happy staff.

Martin rushes things a bit

Martin has advertised his driving school and over the first couple of months he finds himself inundated with prospective learner drivers. He soon sees that he will have to recruit at least three other instructors to work with him, so he puts an advertisement in the local paper. This causes him an additional headache when he receives over 60 replies. Because he is in a big hurry and cannot spend the time sifting through all the applications, he throws out the obvious 'no hopers', but still finds himself left with over 30 applications.

Martin phones them all up and fixes interviews for the following Monday. Only 20 are able to come at such short notice, so he tells the other ten that he will get in touch with them if he does not find the right people at interview.

Unfortunately by the end of Monday, Martin is so confused, having seen so many people in one day, that he is completely incapable of making an objective decision on anyone. In the end he gives the jobs to the three he can remember the best.

Several months later Martin regrets having been so hasty. One of his instructors proves to be most unsatisfactory and begins to give Martin's driving school a bad name.

John finds a new rep

John is really enjoying his new job as sales manager. It means he is largely office based rather than out on the road and this in itself is a whole new experience.

Before John holds his interviews for a new rep, he writes down all the questions he will ask each applicant. He then writes out and learns what he will say about the company and the job on offer. He arranges the interviews over three days, booking just four applicants into each session.

As he appreciates how important it is for sales reps to be good communicators, John decides to introduce some 'play acting' into each interview. He pretends to be an irate customer who has bought a fleet of cars from Gardners Garage and now wants to return them all because they do not do enough miles to the gallon. John assesses very carefully the way each of the applicants handles this situation and from this he is able to make his final decision on who to appoint.

DISCUSSION POINTS

1. How important do you think it is to put a job applicant at ease?

2. What particular characteristics would you look for if you were appointing a teacher for a local comprehensive school?

3. Can you think of any jobs where a slightly big-headed attitude could be an advantage?

6
Appraisal Interviews

Most employees attend appraisal interviews from time to time. Formal interviews are usually held six-monthly or annually, perhaps with less formal chats in between. The **objectives** of appraisal interviews should be:

- to let an employee know that they are valued and cared about

- to improve an employee's performance by using effective communication skills

- to help an employee overcome any failings by discussing problems they may be encountering

- to praise an employee when they have performed well

- to plan an employee's future

- to generate a feeling of teamwork.

Appraisal interviews are not the same as promotion interviews and the two should not be confused. Promotion interviews are discussed in the next chapter.

DOING THE GROUNDWORK

Planning the schedules

Appraisal interviews can be exhausting for both the interviewer and the employee, and if you have planned three or four in one day you are going to regret being so ambitious. Try, if you possibly can, to stagger the appraisals, so that you only interview one member of staff each day. You will then feel alert and capable of dealing with any problems that may arise.

When planning your appraisals give thought to the room you will be using. Make sure it is pleasant to sit in, free from noisy neighbours or continuous interruptions and is private. Choose your time of day carefully too. Just before lunch or home time can set up feelings of resentment before you even start. You might not mind working through the lunch hour or going home late, but your employee might not have the same dedication to duty!

Notifying the relevant members of staff

Appraisal meetings need planning on both sides, so make sure you give plenty of notice to the employees concerned. Ask them to think about their performance over the period in question, and whether they have anything they would particularly like to discuss. Ask them also if the day and time you have chosen is convenient. Try to be accommodating. After all, you want the interview to get off to a good start, and it will not do so if the person sitting opposite you has one eye on the clock because of a prior engagement.

Reading the paperwork

Make sure you prepare well for your appraisal interviews. It is up to you to know every person you interview as well as possible, and you can start to do this by reading through all the paperwork in advance:

- check through the last appraisal, if applicable

- read the personnel files, and find out about any training courses the employee might be involved in

- look at the job description and make sure that the employee is fulfilling the expected role.

Basically, it is your responsibility to read everything you possibly can about the employee you are going to interview, so that both they and you feel able to discuss their performance accurately.

Using an appraisal form

Some organisations use an appraisal form for their interviews. This lists the various jobs that an employee should be carrying out and leaves a space for the interviewer to tick the standard the employee has achieved. It often also gives a space for personal comments relating specifically to each individual employee.

Advantages
- The forms provide a written record of the interview.

- They show the performance of an employee for future reference.

- They provide a quick reference to see where improvement is necessary.

- They enable future targets to be recorded.

Disadvantages
- They can limit discussion at the interview to just the points listed on the form.

- They can intimidate the interviewee if there is a considerable number of negative comments.

- They may encourage a tendency to harp on the past rather than the future, *ie* the ticks apply to what has happened rather than to what could happen.

Drawing up an outline plan

If you are using an appraisal form you will know at least some of the questions you are going to ask the employee. Otherwise, write them out and study them until you feel comfortable asking them.

When you know you are going to have to reprimand someone for failing to reach the required standard, decide beforehand what you are going to say in order to emphasise your dissatisfaction. Do not allow sentiment to creep in. No organisation today can carry 'passengers', and everyone should know that they have their duties to fulfil in a satisfactory manner.

CONDUCTING THE INTERVIEW

Starting with a friendly welcome

Even if you know the interview is going to be difficult because you are not satisfied with an employee's performance, you should still greet them in a pleasant way. After all, they may have a very good reason for their poor performance, and even if they do not, you should still be aiming to act in a positive way to improve things, rather than make them feel uncomfortable as soon as they enter the room.

Show your colleague to a comfortable chair and offer them some refreshment such as tea or coffee. Sit yourself down close by and try to look casual rather than official.

Above all, never give the impression that what is to follow is going to feel like an endurance test. The interview should be a constructive occasion with both sides benefiting from what is discussed.

Establishing the purpose
Start the interview by exchanging pleasantries and then, as soon as possible, explain the purpose of meeting together. Make sure the employee knows what is to be discussed and emphasise that he or she will have ample opportunity to voice any problems or questions.

Begin the interview by giving an overview of the employee's performance during the period in question, and ask if they agree with your overall assessment. Once both sides know the basics more specific points can be discussed.

Discussing any problems or weaknesses
It is an unfortunate fact that appraisal interviews rarely proceed completely smoothly, with the interviewer patting the employee on the back and saying how absolutely perfectly he or she has been performing. Usually there will be at least one or two problems to resolve and, painful though it may be, this is the time to bring things out into the open. Everything said at an appraisal interview should remain **strictly confidential** and difficulties can be aired without embarrassment on either side.

Problems may include:

- unacceptable behaviour towards yourself and/or other colleagues (but not at this stage serious enough to necessitate a disciplinary interview)

- poor timekeeping

- lack of ability

- lack of effort

- failure to reach expected targets.

Remember to 'keep your cool' at all times. Nothing will be gained by shouting at one another, or by you delivering such an onslaught that your employee immediately clams up and says nothing.

Five steps to solving problems
1.   Identify the problem. Get it clear in both your minds what it is that is causing worry.

2.   Look at possible solutions.

3.   Decide between yourselves on the action to be taken.

4.   Take the appropriate action.

5.   Assess whether the problem has been solved. If not, try another possible solution.

Obviously only steps 1–3 can be taken at the interview. Step 4 should be taken immediately afterwards, and step 5 will usually be discussed informally some time in the future, or else at the next appraisal interview.

Giving praise where praise is due
Every one of us has *some* good points and these should be acknowledged. Even if the employee's overall performance has been poor, there should still be something you can praise, just to show that you are not always out to find fault.

It is surprising how much effect even a little praise can have on an employee's performance. We all like to be valued and recognised, especially when we have made a special effort to do our job well. None of us is perfect and we all make mistakes, but a few encouraging words now and again will work wonders for morale boosting.

Agreeing future targets
Not all employees work to targets in the sense of sales type targets, where certain figures must be reached by a given date. All employees can, however, benefit from having some goal or target in mind to achieve within a given period. This may be something very straightforward such as managing to increase their output of correspondence by preparing two extra letters each day, or something complicated such as generating a certain percentage of extra business as each week progresses, resulting in say a 20 per cent increase over a six month period.

Whatever type of targets you have in mind, make sure you both agree on them at the appraisal interview. Be prepared to listen to your employee, in order to ensure that the targets you are setting are realistic. You might, for instance, tell your salesman he must sell ten cars a week for the next six months, but your salesman might turn round and say that this is a totally unrealistic request, perhaps with good cause!

Always remember that most employees will have their own targets too. Ask them about their hopes and ambitions for the future. After all, if someone wants to work hard and climb the ladder to success, you should be encouraging them and advising on how they can best achieve their aims.

Summarising the discussion
By the time an appraisal interview draws to a close, both of you should know exactly what is going to happen next. You will achieve this by handling the interview properly, asking appropriate questions and, even more importantly, listening to what is being said to you. Make sure you have given ample opportunity for discussion on every important point, and that both of you are happy with the outcome.

Summarising the main points of the interview before the employer leaves will reinforce the main points discussed and will give both of you a framework from which to work. Any changes to be made should be especially emphasised so that they are implemented immediately rather than forgotten until the next appraisal interview.

FOLLOWING UP

Preparing a written report
If you have used an appraisal form then all the information can be entered either during or after the interview. Otherwise, it may be a good idea to prepare a written report on the interview, summarising all the main points discussed and any future action to be taken. A copy can then be sent to the employee so that he or she is in no doubt about the outcome of the interview.

Making sure agreed changes are implemented
As we have already said, it is no good agreeing at the interview to make various changes and then completely forgetting about them afterwards. It is up to you to ensure that these changes are implemented by the date agreed.

Checking on progress
It is also your responsibility to ensure that any necessary progress is maintained. Sometimes employees have very good intentions at first, but then they gradually slip back into their old ways. Keep checking and watching; as soon as you feel there is a problem, tackle the person and voice your worries.

Constant supervision is far more important than the formal six-monthly or yearly interview. If employees are monitored carefully, there should be very few adverse comments to make at the appraisal interview and the time can be spent on positive planning for the future.

QUESTIONS AND ANSWERS

Do I need to hold formal appraisal interviews when I chat to my employees all the time about their progress?
Yes. The advantage of a formal interview over a chat is that everything will be discussed and documented in a logical way, so that both of you can refer to it whenever necessary. Matters discussed in the corridor or whilst working can sometimes be forgotten; in any case, almost all employees like the opportunity to talk about their job and their aspirations for the future in private rather than with other colleagues listening in.

Everyone dreads my appraisal interviews because they say they are boring. How can I make them more interesting?
Add some humour and light relief occasionally. Also, encourage your employees to contributed more to the interview themselves and be prepared to deviate from your set questions from time to time. An employee who has sat through the same format appraisal interview every six months for five years *will* be bored, and it is up to you to vary the proceedings.

Can an appraisal interview be used for promotion too?
Yes, but it is far better to hold the interviews separately, so that employees do not think a good appraisal automatically means a promotion.

CHECKLIST

Before
• Have you given thought to why you are holding appraisal interviews?

• Have you planned your interview schedules?

• Have you chosen a suitable place and time for the interview?

• Have you given sufficient notice to the relevant members of staff?

- Have you read all the relevant paperwork?

- Are you using an appraisal form?

- Have you decided on the matters to be discussed at the interview?

During
- Have you shown a friendly welcome?

- Have you established the purpose of the interview?

- Have you discussed any problems and come up with some solutions?

- Have you given praise where praise is due?

- Have you agreed future targets?

- Have you summarised the discussions?

After
- Have you filled in the appraisal form or prepared a written report?

- Have you made sure that changes are implemented and progress is being maintained?

CASE STUDIES

Alex is becoming a bore
Alex has been holding appraisal interviews for 30 years and they have varied very little in that time. All his employees know exactly what to expect the minute they walk through the door, and the interview progresses with both sides going through the motions and Alex filling in his form. In fact most of the workers have learned that they will not get the chance to say very much anyway.

A typical interview runs as follows:

Alex   Hello John. Come in and sit down. Now, appraisal time again. How do you think you have performed over the last year?
John   Well, generally okay, but...
Alex   Jolly good. No worries there then. I'll tick 'satisfactory

performance'. Now, what about promotion? Would you like to be promoted, John?

John   I ... I'm not really sure. It depends what I was offered.

Alex   Yes, quite. I'll tick 'don't know' for that one. I'm quite happy with you anyway. Same time, same place next year then, John.

Alex chuckles to himself as he shows poor John out of the room.

Nicky sets her standards

Nicky is running her first appraisal interviews. She is a high flyer herself and wants to encourage all her workers as much as she can. She prepares an interview plan to use, as follows:

1. Ask how they see their performance over the year.
2. Say how I have seen them performing.
3. Ask about any problems or worries they may have.
4. Tell them about any worries I have.
5. Discuss any changes to take place.
6. Talk about their hopes and ambitions for the future.
7. Tell them their future within the company.
8. Ask for their co-operation to continue to build up the company business.
9. Thank them for all their hard work over the past year and praise any specific 'highs'.
10. Tell them they are valued highly and that I enjoy working with them.

With a positive plan like this Nicky is going to have productive appraisal sessions with all of her staff and can look forward to their co-operation and loyalty in the future.

DISCUSSION POINTS

1. Do you think that appraisal forms are a good idea? Give the reasons for your answer.

2. In your opinion, are staff valued highly enough by their employers?

3. How do you think you can make your appraisal interviews interesting, informative and constructive for everyone who attends them?

7
Promotion Interviews

Promotion interviews frequently have links with both appraisals and job selection interviews. For instance, an employer could decide to promote an employee internally following a successful appraisal, or that employee might find themselves competing with people from outside the organisation for an advertised position, by attending a job selection interview along with everyone else.

It obviously saves both time and money to promote from within whenever possible. It is also good for **staff morale** and **motivation** if people can be seen to be climbing up through the ranks. On the other hand, whenever there is doubt about an internal applicant's suitability for the position on offer, outsiders should be brought in for interview to make sure that the best person for the job is eventually chosen.

Advantages of promoting from within

- Saves time and money.

- Good for staff morale.

- The person already knows the organisation.

- You already know the person.

- You will stand more chance of knowing that person's capabilities.

- There is less risk of them leaving to pursue other interests.

Disadvantages of promoting from within

- Familiarity can be a problem if it causes a biased judgement to be made.

- The promotion of one person could cause jealousy amongst other members of staff.

DOING THE GROUNDWORK

Deciding who to consider

In an ideal world, a job becomes vacant or a new job is created, and someone already working for you fits the bill exactly. No problem. You offer them the job and everyone is happy. Unfortunately, in reality this does not often happen. What is far more likely is that the *wrong* person will seek promotion, and you then have to try very hard to persuade them that perhaps they would be better off staying put for the time being. You will not always succeed, of course, in which case you must let them apply along with, hopefully, some more suitable candidates.

It is up to you to look around and decide who *you* think would be a suitable choice for promotion. Be careful not to fall into the trap of thinking that because someone is very good at the job they are doing, they will automatically be good at another job, because this is not always the case. Check their current job description against the new one and see whether the increased responsibilities should be within their capabilities.

Contacting the persons involved

When you have made your choice or choices, contact the people concerned, either in writing or face to face, and ask them if they are interested in promotion. Talk to them about the new job and make sure they understand exactly what would be expected of them. Be patient if they ask for time to think it over, and also try to understand if they say they are not interested at all. A great many people are very good at the job they do, but have no desire to be promoted to anything better. They are quite happy as they are, and it seems a great shame that in many organisations a lack of ambition is frowned on. After all, workers are needed at every level in the business world, and just think what would happen if we all wanted to become managing directors of large successful companies – the majority of us would quickly become very bitter and disappointed!

Once you know who you are inviting for the promotion interview, you can send out letters giving the day and time. When external applicants are being interviewed too, the interview schedules will need to be carefully planned to ensure that everyone has an equal opportunity for success.

Reading relevant personnel files

Before the interview takes place, read as much as you can about the internal applicants from their personnel files. In particular check to see if they have problems with:

- the way they do their present job

- communicating with other people

- health or their personal life

- discipline

- timekeeping.

If you do find anything untoward, attempt to find out the reasons before the interview takes place.

CONDUCTING THE INTERVIEW

Using the right approach
When external job applicants are involved, it is very important to ensure that you do not give your own employees any special treatment. The object of the exercise is to choose the best person for the job, and you must not allow sentiment or personal bias to get in the way of that objective.

Over-familiarity should be avoided too. Conduct the interview in exactly the same way as you would any other job selection interview. Be friendly, helpful and reassuring but be careful that the interview does not dissolve into a good old 'chit chat'.

Explaining the promotion on offer
Just because a person already works in your organisation, do not assume that they know all there is to know about the job on offer. Many people work almost in a vacuum, doing their own little bit, and never stopping to think about what someone else is doing.

Explain the job in great detail. In particular tell them:

- the exact duties and responsibilities

- the hours of work

- the pay

- the holiday entitlement

- whom they would be working with

- where they would be working

- what they can expect for the future.

It goes without saying that you should have your prepared list of questions to work through. Listen carefully to the replies, and also make sure you give the applicant the opportunity to ask questions.

Considering their suitability

All the time the interview is progressing you should be making your judgement on the suitability of the applicant for the job. As we have already said, it is no use thinking that because someone does one job well they will naturally excel at another. Be constantly mindful of the applicant's strengths and weaknesses and how these will affect their performance should they be promoted.

When you know someone, it is very easy to make a judgement by using your 'gut feelings' about this person. Although this might turn out to be accurate, you should really try to think unbiased, objective thoughts, so that the decision you reach is a sensible one, based on fact rather than on emotion.

FOLLOWING UP

Coming to a decision

This is perhaps the hardest part of the interview, especially if there are several eminently suitable applicants. Ask yourself the following questions:

- Who do you honestly feel would be the best person for the job?

- Who would be able to change to the new position with the minimum amount of upheaval?

- Who seems the most likely to stay with the organisation for the foreseeable future?

- Who has the most easy-going personality to enable them to get on with their new colleagues?

Hopefully answering these questions will point to one person. If not, you will have to think long and hard before coming to any decision.

Informing the people involved

Once you have made your decision you must let everyone concerned know. First of all speak to the successful applicant, just to make sure that they still want the job, and then, assuming they do, contact everyone else as soon as you possibly can.

Assuming you do promote from within, that person will still need to be notified of the promotion in writing as well. They should also receive a new contract of employment, clearly stating their terms and conditions.

It may be appropriate to contact an external job applicant to fill the position vacated by the successful employee. Someone may have aimed higher but this does not necessarily mean they will be unwilling to settle for less, at least for the time being, so it is always worth asking.

Checking on their progress

Some organisations offer a **trial period** for all new and promoted employees. This can be a good thing for both parties, just in case everything does not work out as it should. There have certainly been cases, for instance, of people being promoted to management, only to find that they much preferred being 'one of the lads' on the factory floor. The company car and extra perks mean nothing to them, if they no longer feel able to go down to the local with their workmates on a Friday evening, because those workmates start treating them as an outsider.

Generally, however, selective promotion does work well and increases job satisfaction all round. Checking on progress will then become a routine matter in just the same way as it is for any other member of staff.

QUESTIONS AND ANSWERS

I have a member of staff in my bank who says he just does not want promotion. He does a good job as a cashier but he should be going further. What should I say to him?

As long as he is doing a good job of work leave him alone. Not everyone is ambitious, which is just as well, otherwise you might end up without any cashiers!

Isn't it always better to fill a managerial position from outside? After all, someone newly promoted from within might not be able to command respect from his fellow workers.

This depends very much on the person you are promoting. If you are confident that they can do the managerial job then you should give them the chance to do so. A good manager, even a newly promoted one, should be able to earn respect if he or she treats the other members of staff in the correct manner.

I seem to be holding promotion interviews often at the moment. Several of my senior staff have left and I am promoting everyone to save time and money in recruiting from outside. The people I am promoting are perhaps not entirely suitable but it seems an easy way out. Do you agree with me?

In short – no. You should only ever promote from within if you are sure that the person you are promoting is right for the job, not just to take the easy way out.

CHECKLIST

Before
- Have you decided on who to consider for promotion?

- Have you contacted them and asked whether they are interested in promotion?

- Have you arranged a suitable day and time?

- Have you read the relevant personnel files?

During
- Do you use the right approach?

- Are you able to explain effectively the job on offer?

- Can you judge the applicant's suitability for the job?

After
- Have you made the right decision?

- Have you informed everyone involved of your decision?

- Are you offering a trial period first?

- Are you monitoring the newly promoted person's progress?

CASE STUDIES

James' 'nice guy' image backfires
James has a vacancy in his department for a general administrator. He tells all the relevant office staff about the vacancy and one of them decides to apply. His boss also asks him to advertise the vacancy in the local paper.

James assures Tina, the girl who applies, that she will almost certainly get the job, but he has to go through the motions of interviewing a few 'outsiders' to please his boss. What he does not bargain for is the unprecedented number of applications he receives. When the CVs come in, James realises that several people will have to be interviewed along with Tina, to be absolutely sure of the right decision.

Although James is responsible for his own hiring and firing, his boss, the marketing director, often sits in on the interviews. When they take place, it is obvious that another girl is far more suitable than Tina, because she has several years' administration experience and is already familiar with the word processing package being installed very soon. James feels awful having to break the news to Tina, especially after almost promising her the job.

It would have paid James not to have talked to Tina quite so openly about her chances of success. In the end she is disappointed and blames James for leading her on.

Phillip finds a manager
Phillip's furniture manager is retiring after 40 years' service. This length of service is not unusual as his department store seems to attract loyal employees and vacancies rarely arise.

For some time Phillip has been watching Greg, the assistant manager in the soft furnishings department. Although only 23, Greg has worked for the store since leaving school at 16, and has proved himself to be a very conscientious and effective worker. He mixes well with everyone and Phillip feels he has earned a manager's position.

Phillips speaks to Greg informally at first, asking him if he would be interested in the promotion. Greg is ecstatic, firstly about being considered for promotion and secondly because the manager's position will give him a higher salary which will be very useful as he has just got married.

A week later a successful promotion interview is held and Phillip has a new furniture manager. He then calls in another member of staff who at present only works part-time and offers her the full-time assistant manager's job in soft furnishings. Within two weeks of the vacancy arising Phillips has the store running smoothly once more, with himself and two members of the staff feeling extremely pleased with life!

DISCUSSION POINTS

1. Do you think that all employees should be expected to advance within the organisation they work for?

2. If two members of your staff try for the same promotion, and one succeeds, what would you say to the unsuccessful applicant?

3. In business today, do you think enough emphasis is placed on promotion from within rather than on outside recruitment?

8
Coaching Interviews

Although there are different schools of thought on the exact meaning of the term 'coaching', for our purposes we will think of it as **one-to-one training**. This may mean coaching or training in the practical sense, *eg* how to use a word processing program. Or the coaching may be theoretical, *eg* how to deal with a difficult customer by using methods x, y and z.

A coaching interview is unlike most other interviews, in that it is normally far less formal, but it is still a type of interview all the same.

Nowadays coaching interviews are often held with a view to NVQs (National Vocational Qualifications) being obtained. NVQs are available in many different subjects and, unlike conventional examinations, they deal with the practical side of working achievements.

DOING THE GROUNDWORK

Identifying the need for coaching
Most, if not all, organisations or individuals need to spend a certain amount of time on coaching, if every employee's **full potential** is to be realised.

Advantages of coaching interviews
- offering the opportunity to improve on poor performance
- offering the opportunity to build on past achievements and successes
- increasing an employee's job satisfaction
- giving the employer a chance to delegate.

Disadvantages of coaching interviews
- can be intimidating on a one-to-one basis. Some people would rather attend a conventional training course
- can be very time-consuming.

As the saying goes, however, 'you get out of life what you put into it', and this is true of effective coaching. By spending some time in the short term, tremendous benefit can be gained, for all concerned, in the long term.

Arranging the interview

Coaching interviews will not normally be organised as far in advance as other types of interviews. It is important, nevertheless, to arrange them when you are able to allow plenty of time, because coaching interviews do not always run according to plan. For instance, if someone doesn't grasp what you are trying to explain to them, you cannot just say 'your time's up' and end the session!

Coaching interviews can be held in a variety of places according to the equipment that needs to be available. For instance, training on a word processing program has to be carried out where there is a computer to use. Pretending a computer is sitting on the desk, and using a theoretical approach, is just not good enough! If at all possible, arrange for your coaching interview to be in a reasonably private place, away from interruptions, so that neither you nor your employee are distracted.

It is often a help to prepare written handouts to use during the coaching interview and to give to the employee at the end. This means they have something to refer back to.

Deciding on the objectives

As the interviewer, you must know what you hope to achieve by holding your coaching interview, otherwise it stands very little chance of success. Your objectives might be:

• to achieve certain targets

• to teach new skills

• to build on existing skills

• to help your employee gain NVQs

• to make your employee feel part of a worthwhile team.

Always check carefully in the relevant personnel files before holding your coaching interview. You will find it very embarrassing trying to teach someone a new skill, only to find that it is not new to them at all. Sufficient homework in advance will eliminate the chance of this situation arising.

CONDUCTING THE INTERVIEW

Explaining the purpose of the interview

At the beginning of your coaching interview, explain to the employee exactly what you are hoping to achieve, or rather what you are hoping that they will achieve. Tell them why it is so important. Let them see that you value their presence in your organisation and say that you would like them to get as much as possible out of their working life by reaching their full potential.

Make sure that if more than one item is to be dealt with at the interview, the employee is aware of this, and take things slowly. Resist the temptation to jump about from one item to another. This will cause confusion and your employee will feel unable to concentrate properly.

Encouraging the interviewee to participate

As with every other type of interview, it is very important that you allow the interviewee the opportunity to participate. Explain or demonstrate a point and then let them try it. Check that they understand what they are doing before moving on to something else. Above all, be patient, particularly when you are dealing with someone who is not too quick to grasp things.

It is also very important to encourage the interviewee to put forward their own ideas and suggestions and for you to listen to them. You may be surprised at just how useful these are. Although you have your own methods, it is just conceivable that these might not always be right for every occasion.

Working out an action plan

Writing out an action plan can be a very positive move on both sides. Coaching interviews are not normally one-offs, but part of a continuing **training programme**. Therefore, if an employee's goals are outlined for a set period, then the coaching interviews can be arranged as and when appropriate. Everyone needs something to work towards if they are to perform well, and the time spent working out an action plan will be time well spent. For instance, to take the example of dealing with customers, the action plan could be set out as shown in Figure 7.

Ending on a positive note

Always end a coaching interview by telling the employee that you are pleased with their efforts, but be honest too, and if they still have

ACTION PLAN

Interview 1 Dealing with customers on the telephone
Items covered:

Interview 2 Dealing with customers in writing
Items covered:

Interview 3 Dealing with customers face to face
Items covered:

Interview 4 Dealing with difficult customers
Items covered:

During the interview the items covered can be filled in and then as the employee puts each one into practice they can tick it off.

Fig. 7. A suggested action plan.

a lot to learn then say so. Always add, however, that you have high hopes and ambitions for them and that you intend to help them just as much as you possibly can.

Remember a positive approach means:

- giving praise where praise is due

- offering encouragement for the future

- showing that you care

- helping out with difficulties.

FOLLOWING UP

Carrying out a follow-up interview

As we have said, it is almost inevitable that a follow-up interview will be necessary. The form that this takes will depend on the type of coaching to be undertaken. At all follow-up interviews, however, it is important to establish the following:

- the progress the employee has made since the last interview

- any problems that have been encountered along the way.

Checking on the success of the action plan

Assuming a properly written action plan has been prepared, it will be easy to check how much has been achieved. If you have been doing your job properly you will be aware of just how successful your employee has been and you will be able to give them your feedback. Ask them for their views too, however, and do not be too impatient if they have experienced difficulties with certain aspects of their work. Again, give praise where praise is due, and do not allow anyone to become demoralised just because everything hasn't gone exactly according to plan.

Agreeing on further challenges

Our action plan on dealing with customers allowed for four interviews to be held. Different criteria will demand different treatment and every coaching situation will need to be worked out individually. Set further challenges whenever possible. Generally speaking, an employee can never have too much coaching and training, unless of course you are worried that they will become a threat to your own job if they are too highly trained!

QUESTIONS AND ANSWERS

What is the point of holding coaching interviews for staff taken on with fixed term contracts?
However long they stay, whilst they are working for your organisation your staff should be shown how to carry out their duties in the most efficient and cost effective way possible. This benefits both them and you. In any case, many fixed term contracts are renewed and these workers could well end up staying longer than many of the permanent staff.

Is it better to send employees on outside group training courses with experts teaching them, rather than try to train them in house whilst they are on the job?
This will obviously depend on the circumstances, but generally people learn far more from one-to-one coaching sessions than they do in a large group.

Should I prepare handouts to use for my coaching interviews?
Again, this will depend on the circumstances. Your employees will, however, probably retain more if you give them something to take away and read at the end of the interview.

CHECKLIST

Before
- Have you established the need for a coaching interview?

- Are you sure in your own mind about what it is to achieve?

- Have you allowed plenty of time for the interview?

- Have you chosen a suitable place?

During
- Have you explained the purpose of the interview?

- Have you given the interviewee a chance to participate?

- Have you worked out an action plan between you?

- Have you ended the first interview on a positive note?

After

• Have you carried out a follow-up interview?

• Have you checked on the success of the action plan?

• Have you given your own feedback?

• Have you shown tolerance for any failures?

• Have you agreed on further challenges?

• Are you pleased with how you are conducting your coaching interviews?

CASE STUDIES

Sarah puts her foot in it

Sarah has a new recruit, a middle-aged lady called Judy who has trained to be a social worker now that her children are grown up. Sarah is a little suspicious of Judy as they are more or less the same age and Sarah is used to dealing with much younger girls. Nevertheless, she calls Judy in for the coaching interview she gives all new recruits.

The interview begins badly with Sarah trying to show her seniority in rank, if not in age. She tells Judy that she is not expecting too much of her at first, being so *junior*, but that she is sure Judy will soon begin to fit in, even though she will be much older than her other colleagues.

Sarah then asks Judy why she left it so late to train, intimating that she will only be doing the job for a few years before giving it up to retire! Judy, quite rightly, takes exception to this.

Undeterred, Sarah goes on to say that she will not waste time explaining about the workings of a geriatric hospital, because no doubt Judy, at her age, will know all about them! Judy retaliates angrily, saying that she should be given the same coaching on the workings of the hospital as everyone else, and that her only knowledge to date was gained during the short time she spent working in one whilst training.

It is quite obvious to all that Sarah is just not interested in spending any of her precious time on Judy. Consequently, by the time the coaching interview ends, Judy has learned absolutely nothing, except how rude and unfeeling her new boss can be. She leaves the room feeling very dispirited and definitely old!

John organises his coaching sessions

Having been a rep himself, if there is one thing John is good at, it is coaching other people. He has a young lad working for him who is new to the sales business and John calls him in one day to tell him about dealing with customers. The conversation proceeds as follows:

John   Come in, Paul. Take a seat. Now, today's session is on dealing with the public. What do you think of the great British public by the way?! (John begins in a general way, designed to put Paul at ease.)

Paul   Well, they're a bit of a mixture really. I like people generally, but some are a bit hard to get on with.

John   Tell me about it. I know just what you mean! Let's talk more specifically then. Working as a rep for Gardners you are going to be talking to very important customers. Those customers have to be nurtured and looked after, otherwise they will take their business elsewhere. The customer is always innocent until proved guilty, Paul. That's what you must always remember. Even if you are sure they are in the wrong you must always give them the benefit of the doubt.

Paul   That must be hard sometimes. I don't mind admitting when I'm in the wrong, so why should they?

John   Let me explain a little to you about customer care, Paul. I've got a video here that we can look at together and then we can chat afterwards. Is that okay with you?

John and Paul settle down for their video and have a constructive discussion afterwards. Paul leaves the interview with no doubts about how he will treat his customers whilst he works for Gardners.

DISCUSSION POINTS

1. Do you see coaching interviews as an important part of business life?

2. Do you think one-to-one training is better than group training?

3. Are you aware of NVQs and do you explain them fully to your employees?

9
Counselling Interviews

The aim of holding a counselling interview is to help an employee
overcome a problem that is worrying them. It can be initiated by the
employer or the employee. In other words the employee may
approach you because they want to discuss a problem, or you may
notice a behavioural change and ask them if they would like to talk
about the cause of this change. It should not be confused with a
disciplinary interview (see Chapter 10) which is held when an
employee needs to be rebuked for some misdemeanour.

Serious counselling is usually carried out professionally. Your
role is to offer a friendly ear for someone to off-load their problems.
If you feel that you are getting out of your depth at any time, then
you should call in the experts.

The problem or problems your employee is experiencing may be
home or work related. Always remember that you are not there to
offer advice or to find solutions. You are there to listen and to try to
help the person help themself.

DOING THE GROUNDWORK

Arranging the interview
One of the difficulties surrounding counselling interviews is that they
do not always fall neatly into an interview schedule. Crises can occur
very quickly and it may not be possible to plan the interview in
advance. You will just have to make the best arrangements you can
in the time available. As in all interview situations, however, if
advance planning is possible then so much the better. Otherwise, it
might be better to arrange a quick chat as soon as the problem
arises, and then to fix a longer time for an interview as soon as
possible afterwards.

Choosing a suitable place
This is particularly important with a counselling interview. The

place you choose should first and foremost be completely **private** and **soundproof**. An employee who is already distressed will be even more so if his or her workmates are able to listen in to your interview. It is also important to find somewhere quiet where both of you can concentrate on the matters being discussed, without being interrupted by the ring of the telephone, or a head being popped round the door at frequent intervals.

Finding out background information
An impromptu interview, as we have already said, will have little preparation. When you do have the time to plan, however, it is a good idea to listen out for any background information you can glean on the person you are to interview. Be very **discreet** if you have to ask questions. Do not betray your employee's confidence by telling other people what is going on. Particularly look out for:

- any internal bickering between the employee and his or her colleagues

- the employee's late arrival or early departure

- signs that the employee has been crying or is especially upset

- any information contained in the personnel file about the employee's home life and family

- comments or remarks made about the employee during the working day.

CONDUCTING THE INTERVIEW

Giving a friendly and welcoming greeting
Your employee will often be feeling pretty desperate by the time they talk to you, so it is vital to start the interview in the right way. Greet them warmly, smile, look interested and concerned, and try to make sure that you both sit together on comfy seats. Use some small talk to put the other person at ease. After all, they need to feel able to trust you, otherwise you are both wasting your time.

Showing you are willing to listen
Always remember that you might be the only person in the world that your employee can confide in. This in itself is a huge responsibility. You should begin the interview with gentle probing

about the problem and then sit back and listen as, hopefully, the whole story begins to pour out.

Withholding advice unless asked for it
Be very, very careful about offering any advice. It can backfire on you. If, for instance, you suggest to James, one of your office workers, that he takes Peter to the pub after work to make up their row, and the outing is a disaster, you will get the blame.

Try to develop the knack of putting all advice into the third person. For instance, 'I knew someone called Sue who had that same problem and she joined the local art classes at college' is much safer than saying, 'Why don't you join the art classes at the college on Wednesday evenings. I could find out about it if you like. That's the sort of thing you need to take you out of yourself.'

Understanding and sympathising
There is a vast difference between showing understanding and sympathy and being patronising. No one likes being patronised or treated like an unfortunate child who is too inadequate to sort their life out.

Remember that what might seem a small problem to you is obviously very important to your employee and it is up to you to help them talk through that problem and reach their own conclusion. Do not take sides and, once again, be very careful with any advice you offer.

Being prepared for an emotional outburst
Some people are very good at coping with tears and tantrums. Others are not so good and quickly feel embarrassed and even frightened. If you know in advance what is bothering your employee you will be better prepared for any outburst during the interview. Should such a situation arise, try the following:

- pass them a hanky

- offer them a break and a cup of tea or coffee

- change the subject for a little while until they have a grip on their emotions once more

- gradually ease the conversation back to the matter in hand

- take comfort from the fact that dramatic emotional outbursts only usually happen once in an interview.

FOLLOWING UP

Seeing if things improve

After the interview has taken place, keep a close watch on your employee. See if they show signs of feeling happier and less stressed than they did before the interview. Miracles are a rare occurrence, however, and it will usually take a little time for someone to sort their life out, so don't be too impatient.

Arranging a follow-up interview

Depending on the circumstances, it is often a good idea to arrange a follow-up interview date at the end of the first interview. This can make the person feel secure in the knowledge that somebody cares about them. Continuing support can be an important part of counselling. A one-off interview is often not enough to sort out the problem once and for all. The person concerned may well want to try various ways of improving things and then report back to you on their progress.

At a follow-up interview remember to ask the following:

• what action they have taken to make things better

• whether they feel that action has worked

• how they feel about the problem now

• any ideas they may have for future improvements

• whether they feel it will be necessary to talk with you again.

Maintaining confidentiality

Your employee has put their trust in you by discussing their troubles. Never let them down and allow that trust to be misplaced. Do not discuss **anything** to do with the interview with anyone else, unless you have the permission of your employee to do so.

QUESTIONS AND ANSWERS

Do I need to do a course in counselling before I hold a counselling interview?

No, not necessarily, unless you are planning to hold them regularly! For one-off situations, a sympathetic ear and the ability to listen and show understanding are the only real prerequisites.

The girl who works for me is going through a marriage break-up. I know this because her husband works for my friend. Should I approach her about this and offer her a counselling interview? Her work does not seem to be suffering at the moment but I'm worried that it could do in the future.
Quite definitely, no! If your assistant wants to talk, she will no doubt approach you, but unless her work is affected you should keep the information you have gained strictly to yourself. A kind word now and then would not go amiss though!

Surely counselling is just a new fancy way of wasting time by dishing out tea and sympathy. Why don't people sort out their own lives rather than expect others to do it for them?
Many people have no one they can turn to in a crisis and they become unable to cope. Counselling an employee in trouble can be beneficial both for them and also for you, in terms of their concentration and commitment at work.

CHECKLIST

Before
• Are you able to plan the interview in advance?

• Have you decided where to hold it?

• Have you thought about confidentiality?

• Have you tried to find out some background information?

During
• Have you welcomed your employee in a friendly way?

• Have you given the impression that you are willing to listen without judgement?

• Have you refrained from giving advice?

• Have you tried to help by talking about someone else in a similar situation?

• Have you shown an understanding and sympathetic approach?

● Have you managed to cope with any emotional outbursts?

After
● Have you kept a close watch on the situation?

● Have you arranged a follow-up interview?

● Have you managed to maintain complete confidentiality?

CASE STUDIES

Phil offers a sympathetic ear

As Station Officer, Phil always likes his men to not only do their job well, but to look happy too. In fact he prides himself on having the happiest Watch in the district. It therefore upsets him greatly to see one of his young lads, Steve, suddenly become serious, miserable and indifferent to everyone around him. He still does his job well but he seems desperately unhappy so Phil asks to see him. The interview runs as follows:

Phil	Hello Steve, thanks for coming along. Sit down over here. Would you like some coffee?
Steve	Er, no thanks Guv. (Steve looks uncomfortable. His boss has asked for the interview and Steve is not sure why, although he does have a fairly good idea.)
Phil	Now, Steve, I'm beginning to get worried about you. Lately you have changed from being one of the liveliest of my lads to one of the quietest. Has someone upset you?
Steve	No, Guv.
Phil	Well, something must be wrong somewhere. Do you want to talk about it?
Steve	It's not to do with work, Guv, so there is no need to involve you. You must have enough problems of your own to worry about.
Phil	I want to see you happy again, Steve. I'm here to try and help you, whatever your problems, so why don't you try me?
Steve	Okay then, but you'll think it's just silly. The thing is my girlfriend, Sue, wants me to give up fire-fighting. She doesn't like me working shifts and wants me to get a nine to five job.
Phil	But what do you want to do? Are you serious about this girl?

Steve	Well, I was, but since all this business, I've begun to wonder. We don't live together or anything like that. She lives with her mum and dad, but we were going to get engaged – or at least she wanted to. (He added the last part as an afterthought.)
Phil	So, do you still enjoy the Brigade, Steve? How would you feel about changing jobs?
Steve	The Brigade is my life, Guv. It's all I've ever wanted, and she should understand that.
Phil	Do you think she's jealous of how much it means to you?
Steve	Probably, yes. It's ridiculous though. Here's me been feeling guilty about wanting to stay in the Brigade rather than do as she wants, and yet if I really stop to think about it, I've had enough of her anyway. (Steve stops and smiles at his boss.) I suppose that solves the problem really, doesn't it, Guv.
Phil	I guess it does, Steve. So will you be looking happier soon?
Steve	Yes, thanks for listening, Guv. Talking to you got it all into perspective for me. I'd been bottling it up for weeks.

By talking it through Steve has solved the problem all by himself, and in this instance Phil is sure that very soon he will see a marked improvement in Steve's behaviour at work.

Sarah throws her weight around

As senior social worker, Sarah takes it upon herself to lecture the younger girls. One of her new social workers, Rachel, asks to see her about a personal matter. Sarah arranges an interview for later in the week. It transpires that Rachel's granny has become very ill and has been taken into a nursing home, more or less on a permanent basis, and although Rachel is used to dealing with elderly people, she is finding it difficult to come to terms with her granny's plight.

Sarah listens to Rachel and then sets about putting matters right:

Sarah	Now, my dear, I know how you must be feeling, but we must be sensible, mustn't we. It happens to us all and you should know that better than most, working in a geriatric hospital.
Rachel	Yes, but I love my granny so much and I hate to see her in pain, and in a strange place.
Sarah	I'm sure you do, but it's all for the best. Now we'll just

have to pull ourselves together, won't we, otherwise our work will begin to suffer and that will never do.

Rachel   No, Mrs Read. Do you think I could have Friday off to go and see her? I would feel better if I can see where she is and my mother is going up there on Friday.

Sarah   No, I don't think that is a good idea, Rachel. We are short-staffed this week and we all have to pull our weight, regardless of our personal problems.

Needless to say, Rachel leaves in tears and absolutely nothing is solved. She still goes on worrying about her granny.

DISCUSSION POINTS

1. Do you think that counselling should only be done by a professional person?

2. 'A problem shared is a problem halved.' Explain your interpretation of this statement.

3. What would you do if your employee told you her marriage was breaking up and she had contemplated suicide?

10
Grievance Interviews

A grievance interview takes place when someone feels that he or she is being unfairly treated, by a colleague, by the boss, or by the workplace in general. The single most important point to remember is that during the interview you **must get to the truth**, and sometimes this can be hard to do.

DOING THE GROUNDWORK

Establishing the circumstances
As a grievance interview is requested by the employee, it should be possible for you to talk to them beforehand so that you are fully aware of what needs to be discussed. Of course, not all grievance matters wait for a formal interview to be arranged. Sometimes a matter needs to be dealt with immediately, but basic interview procedures can still be followed even if you do not have the chance to prepare in full.

Speaking to other members of staff
Remember that the employee who is complaining will be giving you their own view of the prevailing circumstances. It is then up to you to speak to any other relevant members of staff, not saying why at this stage, but just trying to get an overall picture of the person you will be interviewing and any factors that may be contributing to the problem.

Reading the relevant personnel files
Most organisations have personnel files on all their employees. If so, read through everything you can find on the person you will be interviewing. See whether they have had any behavioural problems noted, or if they find it difficult to mix *etc*. All these factors may well be relevant to the interview.

Arranging the interview
Assuming you do have the time to arrange the interview properly, start

by selecting somewhere quiet, pleasant and confidential to hold it.

Confidentiality is even more important here than it is for most interviews, because grievance matters can quickly get out of hand if someone overhears any snippets of the interview taken out of context.

You should also allow plenty of time. The main aim, as we have said, is for you to get to the truth and you will only do this by probing, asking the right questions, listening to the answers, and letting the other person see that you are interested in what they are saying. It takes time to win a person's trust, so you cannot rush this part of the proceedings.

CONDUCTING THE INTERVIEW

Putting the person at ease
The same points apply here as to the counselling interview in Chapter 9. Either your employee may feel nervous and unsure about what they are doing, or they may be just plain angry about whatever has happened to prompt the interview. Whichever is the case, the way you handle the situation during those first few minutes will set the scene for the rest of the interview.

Asking for details of their problem
By now you should have a very good idea of what the problem is, but you probably will not know all the details. Coax your employee to tell you *everything* and listen very carefully to what they say. You will soon be able to form your own opinion on whether or not their complaint sounds justified.

Typical work-related complaints may include:

- being victimised by yourself

- being victimised by a colleague

- being asked to undertake additional extra tasks

- being expected to work unreasonable hours

- receiving inadequate pay and/or benefits

- working with someone who smokes

- working with someone who does not do their share of the job

- working with someone who is causing sexual harassment.

All of these are very valid reasons for complaint, just so long as the allegations are found to be true. It has to be said, however, that some people do look for trouble and their idea of sexual harassment, for instance, might be someone else's idea of being friendly.

Indicating that you intend to help

Whether or not the complaint is, in your opinion, over-exaggerated, you must still show your employee the courtesy of listening and agreeing to help. Be careful not to take sides, but discuss the matter in full detail, restating everything they say to you so that both of you get a clear picture of the situation.

Talking through possible solutions

Let us take the following as an example:

A female member of staff has come to see you because she says that her male colleague keeps telling sexist dirty jokes and making rude remarks about women in general. You may or may not think that he is overstepping the mark depending on the full facts. Let us consider some points which may be relevant:

- On how many occasions has this happened?

- Has the man in question ever proved troublesome before?

- Has the employee ever asked him not to tell these jokes or to be rude about women?

- What has he said in answer?

You will see from the above that the way these questions are answered could make a considerable difference to the allegation, and it is up to you to form your own conclusions and then to offer solutions. If you feel the employee in our scenario is making a lot out of very little, you could say that you will have a word with the man, but that perhaps she could try being slightly less sensitive. On the other hand, if you find out that the man is being a real nuisance, you will need to reprimand him severely, so that he knows that such behaviour will not be tolerated.

Whatever you suggest, make sure that the employee is happy with your suggestion and try to end the interview on a sympathetic note, however you feel about the matter yourself. Show her that you *do* care, you *are* prepared to listen, and that you will always take the appropriate action rather than let a situation get out of hand.

FOLLOWING UP

Interviewing anyone else involved

The vast majority of grievance matters involve more than one person. Apart from practical problems such as workload, hours, pay *etc*, or a complaint against yourself, you will usually need to see someone else after you have interviewed the employee making the complaint, if only to get their side of the story and initiate any action to be taken. It may then be necessary to hold 'all party talks' when all of you get together to discuss what is going to happen next.

Let us take the dirty jokes scenario as an example of successful follow-up.

You have told the employee that you will have a word with Mr Y, so you need to arrange for him to come and see you. When he does, simply explain the situation and, depending on what you have found out, reprimand him accordingly. You might like to also mention that you are sure he would not want to give the female employee any grounds for an official complaint to a tribunal about his sexist remarks. This should do the trick and will probably mean Mr Y will temper his behaviour in the future.

Keeping an eye on the situation

Any matter that an employee feels is serious enough to complain about needs to be monitored. Keep a discreet eye open so that you can see that any measures discussed at the interview are being implemented.

However much you try, you will never stop people complaining. Some of their complaints will be fully justified and some will not, but we are all individuals with very different personalities, and in a working situation personality clashes will almost inevitably occur from time to time.

QUESTIONS AND ANSWERS

I find women so difficult to handle. They are so emotional about everything. How can I hold a grievance interview if they keep crying

all the time? I just lose my temper.
Women do not cry *all* the time. They only cry if they are provoked, so if you behave decently to them, it is just possible that they will respond accordingly. Give them a chance to explain their problem, and treat them with sympathy and respect. It is true, you may encounter the occasional emotional female, but some men are emotional too, you know!

What is the difference between a grievance interview, a counselling interview and a disciplinary interview?
A grievance interview is initiated by an employee because he or she has a work-related complaint to make. A counselling interview can be initiated by either an employer or employee because of the employee's personal problem, which may be affecting the person's working ability and/or general behaviour. A disciplinary interview is initiated by the employer when an employee needs to be reprimanded for some misdemeanour committed at work.

How can I tell if someone is telling the truth at a grievance interview?
The more experience you have in interviewing the easier you will find it to judge. See if the person looks you in the eye and whether their story sounds true. If in doubt, check the facts.

CHECKLIST

Before
- Do you know the reason why your employee has asked for a grievance interview?

- Are you prepared to respond to their request in a positive way?

- Have you read the relevant paperwork and tried to glean information from other members of staff?

- Have you arranged the interview at a convenient time and in a suitable, confidential place?

During
- Have you managed to settle the employee down?

- Have you asked for full details of the problem?

- Have you impressed upon them the need to tell the truth?

- Have you indicated that you are prepared to help?

- Have you talked through possible solutions?

After
- Have you interviewed anyone else involved?

- Have you listened to their side of the story?

- Have you taken the appropriate action?

- Are you going to carry on monitoring the situation?

CASE STUDIES

Phil has a female problem

Phil is approached one day by his only female fire-fighter, Suzy. Suzy asks for a grievance interview to be arranged in order to discuss the victimisation she feels she is receiving from one of the other fire-fighters.

During the interview Suzy tells Phil that Robert, the fire-fighter in question, has been rude about her ever since she joined the Watch. Phil asks for more details and Suzy gives him plenty of examples including one incident when he deliberately sprayed deodorant all over her clothes, and another when he swore profusely at her just for being a woman doing what he considered to be a man's job.

Phil checks out Suzy's allegations by talking discreetly to other members of the Watch, and he soon learns that they are all true. Absolutely furious, he then interviews Robert and gives him a very stern warning, saying that he will be reported to higher authority if his behaviour does not improve. He tells Robert that Suzy is a first-class fire-fighter and that his is proud to have her as part of the Watch. He also says that if someone has to go, it will not be her.

Although Robert continues to make the odd jibe, he does try to be more civil to Suzy and things settle down once more. Phil continues to monitor the situation for some time and asks Suzy to tell him immediately any more trouble starts. Thankfully this does not prove to be necessary.

Alex shows his usual tact and diplomacy

One of Alex's admin staff has asked for a grievance interview to discuss the fact that he is being asked to work unreasonable hours.

The interview runs as follows:

Alex Hello, John – take a seat. Now what's all this about your working hours. Not having another moan, are you? (Alex starts the interview by making John feel he is wasting his time.)

John Look, Mr Jones, I don't mind working overtime. I've done it for long enough after all. But now I'm being asked to come in at weekends too and my wife is complaining. It just isn't fair.

Alex I expect your wife likes the overtime payments though, doesn't she? Gives you some money to take her out for a drink once in a while, eh?

John My wife doesn't drink and as we have two young children she would far rather me be there with her at weekends than have a little extra money. It's the only time we have together.

Alex Dear, dear, my heart bleeds for you. Well, I'll see what I can do. Can't promise anything though, and don't forget with the present recession you're lucky to have a job at all. There are plenty more out there to take your place...

And so he continues, leaving John feeling totally dissatisfied with the entire interview. Things won't change because Alex doesn't want them to and the situation will just worsen as each week goes by. John will become increasingly unhappy and start to look around for another job. He is a very good worker and it will be Alex's loss in the end.

DISCUSSION POINTS

1. How would you handle an interview with a very tearful, emotional female, who insists she is being victimised by her work colleagues because she wears glasses, when you know that her allegations are unfounded?

2. 'It's too easy nowadays for someone to complain.' Explain your feelings on this statement.

3. What special skills do you think an interviewer needs in order to successfully conduct a grievance interview?

11
Disciplinary Interviews

A disciplinary interview is one of the least pleasant types of interview to conduct. It is initiated by the employer and is necessary when a member of staff has acted in a way that is unacceptable to you or to the organisation you represent. As with a grievance interview, the most important aim is to get to the truth.

If you are the type who likes to be liked you may be worried that you will end up making enemies, and dread disciplinary interviews for that reason. By conducting the interview in the correct manner, however, you should be able to portray yourself as a fair and just person who is trying to work in a positive way to put things right.

DOING THE GROUNDWORK

Following company procedures
Most organisations have set rules for dealing with certain procedures such as dismissal, redundancy, poor timekeeping, absence from work, and health and safety requirements. These will normally be laid down in the **staff handbook** and/or the **contract of employment**. There are also certain legal requirements that you should be aware of. Make sure you check all relevant points carefully before beginning any disciplinary proceedings.

Collecting the evidence
There is nothing more embarrassing than instigating a disciplinary interview and then finding out that you were wrong in your interpretation of the situation.

For instance, you may decide to hold such an interview because you have seen one of your employees arriving late for work every morning for two weeks. This, you think to yourself, cannot continue and so, rather than speak to the departmental manager first, you fix a date and time for the person to come and see you. At the interview the employee points out that she had asked her manager about taking the time off, which was necessary for her to have daily checks at the local hospital for a blood condition. In this situation it is your departmental manager who is at fault for not keeping you informed, but you are at fault too for not investigating the facts before summoning the employee. The one person who is blameless is the employee you are disciplining!

This little example serves to emphasise that it is vitally important to speak to other people, read personnel files, and do some digging to make absolutely sure of your facts *before* arranging such an interview.

Making notes

Although we always hope for a positive outcome, it is possible that a single disciplinary interview will not be the end of the matter. For this reason, as well as to refresh your memory when the interview takes place, make copious notes on all the information you think is relevant, and keep those notes in a file.

Organising a suitable time and place

This is going to be a tricky interview for all concerned, so the timing is particularly important. The best options are either:

- towards the end of the working day so that the person can go home afterwards, or

- at the end of the working week – for instance, if the person works from Monday to Friday, Friday afternoon would probably be favourite.

The venue for the interview is important too. As with all interviews, you will need to find somewhere quiet, but with disciplinary interviews it is particularly important to also ensure that your session will be held in complete confidence. It is not your reputation at stake but that of your employee's, and you should respect that fact at all times.

Informing the person involved

Some disciplinary interviews, for serious misconduct, will have to be held immediately, with little or no notice on either side. If possible, however, and under normal circumstances, give plenty of notice, so that the employee has adequate time to prepare for what is ahead, and to get together their own defence.

Arranging for witnesses to attend

Again the seriousness of the situation will dictate whether or not **witnesses** need to be present. If they are required make sure they have plenty of notice, and should the suggested day and time not be convenient, re-schedule the interview rather than manage without them.

CONDUCTING THE INTERVIEW

Greeting the employee

Even though you have arranged the interview because you are unhappy about a person's performance, you should still start out by giving them the benefit of the doubt. Greet them pleasantly and assure them that your interview will be strictly confidential.

Disciplinary interviews can be very emotional on both sides, so you should be prepared for this. On no account should you lose your temper, even if provoked, for this will solve nothing at all.

Outlining the subjects for discussion

As soon as you have exchanged brief pleasantries, explain the purpose of the interview and outline the subjects to be discussed. This is not usually a surprise to either side because the normal procedure is to tell the employee what the interview will be about at the time it is arranged.

Remember at all times to be objective in your discussions. It is important not to let any of the following get in your way:

- a clash of personalities

- personal bias for a reason that is not relevant to the present discussions

- hearsay from other people which is based on supposition rather than fact.

Reiterating previous warnings

It is, of course, possible that this is not the first disciplinary procedure to be taken against your employee. They may have attended a previous interview, or they may have already received a written warning about their behaviour. In either case, always reiterate the content of these warnings before proceeding with the interview.

Allowing time for explanations

Always keep in your mind the three main purposes of the interview:

1. to get to the truth
2. to positively discuss the matter between you
3. to put matters right.

A disciplinary interview which later leads to dismissal is not what you are out to achieve, and for this reason alone you must give your employee adequate opportunity to explain their side of the story. Do not allow an argument to develop. There is a vast difference between a constructive discussion and an argument. The latter is counterproductive.

Giving time-scales for improvement

Once the situation has been fully discussed and you have given the employee clear guidelines on the improvement you require, time-scales should be set, otherwise things will tend to drift as before once the interview ends. These time-scales should be realistically worked out. For instance, if someone has been struggling to perform well, an unrealistic time-scale for improvement will put them off before they even begin their reforming process.

Summarising the discussion

As the interview proceeds you should once again be making notes, but try not to make these look too official, otherwise the other person may clam up. At the end of the interview you should be able to use these notes to summarise the proceedings for you both. Make absolutely sure that your employee knows:

- what they need to do to rectify the unacceptable situation

- how soon they are expected to show significant improvement

- that you are there to help if they run into difficulties

- that you are not going to tolerate the present situation and that if no improvement is made further action will be taken.

Try to end the interview on a positive note by saying that you are sure everything will run smoothly in the future – even if deep down you are not at all sure!

FOLLOWING UP

Keeping a close check on the situation

After the interview it is up to you to continue monitoring the situation carefully. Again, make notes on what happens next, and keep these, along with all the other notes, in case they are needed in the future. Ask other people who work with the person in question and take notice of their feedback. In other words, make sure you are aware of what is going on.

Arranging follow-up interviews

You may have chosen to arrange a follow-up interview in order to reassure your employee that they are not going to be forgotten. On the other hand, you may be forced to arrange a follow-up interview because the person's performance fails to improve.

Taking further action

In the latter case, after the follow-up interview, you may find it necessary to send a formal written warning to the employee, so that the situation is on record for all to see. After all, by the time a follow-up interview and a written warning are felt to be necessary, the situation has obviously become quite serious and any future dismissal proceedings will need to be supplemented by documentary evidence. Whilst dismissal should always be thought of as the very last resort, you must cover yourself, just in case there is no other way out.

QUESTIONS AND ANSWERS

I hate holding disciplinary interviews in case the person is nasty to me. Can't I just send them a letter and have done with it?
A letter only gives your side of the story. It is important to interview the person to try to understand the reasons behind their unsatisfactory behaviour.

What happens if the person I am interviewing loses their temper and starts to shout at me? Should I shout back?
Absolutely not. Two wrongs do not make a right. Ask them politely to quieten down, saying that nothing will be gained from tempers being lost. Then continue with the interview, in the best way that you can, and remember to note the loss of temper, to alert you for any further interviews.

I prefer an informal chat to a proper disciplinary interview. This gives me the chance to sort things out over a pint or a game of golf. Is this okay?
Everyone has their own way of dealing with such matters and your way is not *necessarily* wrong. The problem arises if things do not

improve and you then have to become heavy-handed. This is harder to do when you have treated the person as a 'pal'.

CHECKLIST

Before
• Have you checked on company procedures?

• Are you sure that what you are arranging conforms to these?

• Have you done your research?

• Are you sure the interview is necessary?

• Are you keeping notes on everything?

• Have you chosen a suitable time for the interview?

• Have you given the employee ample notice?

• Have you notified any witnesses who may be involved?

During
• Have you welcomed the employee in an appropriate manner?

• Have you outlined the subjects for discussion?

• Have you drawn attention to any previous warnings?

• Have you allowed the other person time to explain their side of the story?

• Have you given time-scales for improvement?

• Have you summarised the discussions and ended on a positive note?

After
• Are you continuing to monitor the situation carefully?

• Have you arranged any necessary follow-up interviews?

- Have you been forced to take further disciplinary action?

CASE STUDIES

Martin gets taken in

One of Martin's driving instructors, Roger, has failed to perform well almost since day one. He is rude to the other instructors and often to Martin himself. None of the clients has ever complained, but Martin is sure that it is only a matter of time before one of them does. Roger's driving skills are excellent and all of his clients have passed their test first time, so he has hesitated to say anything.

After one particularly upsetting incident when Sheila, a female instructor, is accused by Roger of poaching one of his clients, Martin steps in and arranges a disciplinary interview.

One of Martin's problems is that he likes being popular and tries never to make any enemies. He therefore begins the interview on the defensive saying how sorry he is to have to speak to Roger about his behaviour, and that he is sure there is a perfectly logical explanation for the attitude Roger takes sometimes. Roger, being rather clever and sensing an opportunity to get out of this tricky situation, says that he has not been feeling himself lately because of a personal problem and that he never takes this out on the clients, but sometimes the other staff may have had to bear the brunt.

Martin is soft-hearted and immediately feels sorry for Roger. The interview is brought abruptly to a close when Roger promises to try harder in future, and both men feel very pleased with their achievements.

Unfortunately for Martin, Roger was lying, and things go from bad to worse. The clients start complaining about his behaviour too, and Martin becomes desperate. Had he handled the disciplinary interview effectively, maybe the problem could have been nipped in the bud, but now Martin is faced with giving formal written warnings and beginning dismissal proceedings.

Sonia gives a timekeeping reprimand

Despite repeated reprimands, one of Sonia's receptionists, Rosemary, manages to turn up late for every shift, whether morning, afternoon or evening. Annoyed that her reprimands are being ignored Sonia arranges a disciplinary interview.

Sonia begins by refreshing Rosemary's memory about the purpose of the interview. She goes on to ask why her various reprimands have been ignored. Rosemary shrugs her shoulders and says she didn't think that Sonia *really* minded just so long as there were plenty of other staff on duty, and all her workmates knew that she sometimes had problems getting in on time because of her little boy.

Sonia makes it perfectly plain that she is not prepared to tolerate this behaviour any more, and that unless Rosemary's timekeeping improves, further disciplinary action will be taken without any hesitation.

By the time the interview ends Rosemary knows exactly where she stands. Either she turns up on time or she is going to be in big trouble. As a single parent she feels she is being unfairly treated but realises that she is going to receive no sympathy from Sonia.

DISCUSSION POINTS

1. 'Effective management should remove the need for disciplinary interviews.' Discuss this statement.

2. What do you see as the main difference between disciplinary interviews and counselling interviews?

3. Do you feel it is important to speak to somebody about their performance at work before putting your feelings in writing?

12
Dismissal Interviews

There is no way of hiding the fact that dismissal interviews are traumatic occasions. Emotions run high. It is the end of the road for the employee and the interviewer has the unpleasant task of telling them so. The job has to be done, however, and it is in everyone's interest to do it in the most efficient and least painful way possible.

DOING THE GROUNDWORK

Collating all relevant information
If a person has been caught stealing the company funds, sexually assaulting a secretary, or committing other equally horrendous offences then he or she can be sacked without warning or notice. In such cases you would have to carry out your dismissal interview without preparation. Such cases are, however, in the minority.

Normally, before dismissing anyone, you need to show by means of **documentary evidence** that you have tried all available means to correct a person's behaviour and that all those attempts have failed. At least one verbal warning (a disciplinary interview) and two written warnings should be given to the employee. The written warnings state the facts as they are, and copies must always be kept on file for use at the dismissal interview. All this paperwork needs to be collated, together with any reports from other members of staff, before the interview takes place, so that you are absolutely sure of your facts.

Checking on employees' rights
Until the early 1970s it was possible for an employer to dismiss an employee without any reason at all, so long as the employee received adequate notice. Even the notice could be waived if the employee was found to be in breach of his or her contract of employment or the rules in the staff handbook.

The Industrial Relations Act (1971) changed all that by

introducing **unfair dismissal**. This in simplified terms means that if employees feel they are being dismissed for no valid reason they can appeal to an industrial tribunal.

No employer wants the hassle of an unfair dismissal claim, so it is very important to make sure that the dismissal interview is conducted in such a way as to ensure that all the employee's rights are covered. This means having documentary evidence of the reason for dismissal, giving adequate notice or pay in lieu of notice, and taking care of any other entitlements such as holiday pay, pension fund provision *etc*.

If you are to be involved in dismissal interviews it is a good idea to acquaint yourself with the current employment law. There are many detailed books on the subject, one of the easiest to understand being *Employment Law* by Christopher Waud, published by Michael O'Mara Books.

Informing the person of the interview time
As by now dismissal is inevitable, there is no need to give too much notice of the interview day and time. It is a good idea to arrange the interview for the end of a working day or week, however, so that the employee can slide off home afterwards rather than have to face colleagues.

Arranging for witnesses to be present
Where the employee belongs to a union, it is usual to invite the union leader along to the interview so that fair play can be witnessed. Additionally, you may wish to have a member of staff attend to witness your side of the interview. It goes without saying that any witnesses should be told that the matters discussed are strictly confidential and are not to be divulged to anyone else after the interview.

CONDUCTING THE INTERVIEW

Ensuring the interview is correctly conducted
Employment law today really protects the employee more than the employer and this fact should always be borne in mind. Never say or do anything that could be misinterpreted and used against you. Stick to the rules and keep the interview as brief as possible.

Outlining previous disciplinary action
In order to build up your case for dismissal, it is important for you

to outline all previous disciplinary action. Show copies of written warnings and notes of disciplinary interviews. Reiterate all the circumstances leading to dismissal.

Explaining the reason for dismissal

However many mitigating circumstances there are, you must still spell out the exact reason for dismissal. For instance:

> You are being dismissed because you have on 15 occasions over the last two months failed to turn up for work with no reason being offered in your defence. This has been discussed with you at two disciplinary interviews and you have also received two written warnings. Despite these warnings your unsatisfactory conduct has continued and therefore dismissal is our only course of action.

Remember to state the exact date you expect the employee to leave.

Showing your regret at the decision

Although by now you may be relieved that perhaps many months of disciplinary proceedings are at last over, you will probably still feel a tinge of regret that the situation has ended this way. Even if you don't you should still indicate to your employee that you are sorry about what has happened. It may help to close by saying that you hope they manage to find employment elsewhere in a place where they feel able to give of their best. On the other hand, if you think the person is likely to punch you on the nose if you come out with such a statement, just express your regret and leave it at that!

FOLLOWING UP

Checking on relevant pay and documents

When an employee is dismissed you will need to check on the following:

- any pay they are entitled to

- any outstanding holiday entitlement

- tax and national insurance documents

and, if applicable:

• pension fund contributions

• staff social club contributions

• company car.

You are also required by law to give the employee a **written statement** stating the reasons for dismissal.

Making sure everyone else is told

Dismissing someone always leaves a rather bitter feeling, even if everyone knows that he or she deserved it. It is vital that you speak to any other staff who worked with the person and explain, briefly, that the person has been dismissed. You may or may not feel it is necessary to give the specific reasons why. Often these reasons are general knowledge anyway.

Make it clear to your other employees that dismissal was not a decision you took lightly, but that you are not prepared to tolerate unsatisfactory conduct from any member of staff. This will set the record straight for the future.

QUESTIONS AND ANSWERS

I'd hate to be taken to an industrial tribunal and have to pay lots of money for unfair dismissal. How can I avoid this happening?
Obviously reasons for dismissal will be interpreted in different ways. An employee might genuinely feel unfairly treated however careful you are. All you can do is try to make sure that you are definitely justified in making your decision and that you have the documentary evidence to back you up. Then, even if you are taken to a tribunal you should be able to win your case.

I feel I have failed when I am forced to dismiss someone. Should I feel this way?
There are occasions when disciplinary procedures are handled badly and employees end up without a job simply because of bad management of the situation. Such occasions are rare, however, and so long as you feel you have dealt with the situation in the right way you should have a clear conscience.

I have proof that one of my members of staff has been fiddling the books for three months now. He must have made himself at least £3,000. Can I dismiss him without notice?

So long as you have proof then yes. You must also consider taking relevant proceedings against him to recover the money.

CHECKLIST

Before
- Is dismissal the only option?

- Are you familiar with current employment law?

- Have you gathered the relevant information?

- Have you checked on the employee's rights?

- Have you informed the person of the interview day and time?

- Have you thought about whether witnesses should be present?

During
- Are you sure that you are conducting the interview correctly?

- Have you outlined previous disciplinary action?

- Have you spelt out the exact reason for dismissal?

- Have you shown that you regret dismissing the person?

After
- Have you checked out the paperwork, including pay and tax/NI documents?

- Have you informed the rest of the staff and let them see that you will not stand any nonsense from them either?

CASE STUDIES

Sonia shows she means what she says

Rosemary the errant receptionist has now received two written and two oral warnings about her poor timekeeping. There has been no improvement at all so Sonia decides that dismissal is the only answer.

At the interview Sonia explains exactly why she is dismissing Rosemary and that she would like her to accept one month's pay in lieu of notice. Rosemary acts as though she really couldn't care less and tells Sonia that she will easily be able to get a much better job anyway, with higher pay and more sociable hours. Sonia wishes her the best of luck and agrees with Rosemary that she was obviously not suited to the health centre and will probably be happier elsewhere.

Rosemary flounces out and Sonia heaves a sigh of relief!

Martin digs himself a hole

Since the disciplinary interview was held Martin has not actually got around to issuing any written warnings to Roger, his bad mannered driving instructor, but he has just about had enough of his bad behaviour. At first he was taken in by Roger's explanation of having some personal problems, but the situation has deteriorated to such an extent that Roger has managed to upset at least six of their clients as well as all the other driving instructors.

Martin calls Roger in one morning and, without further warning, dismisses him. Roger says he can't do that without the customary number of warnings, but Martin is desperate and just wants to be rid of this awful man. He offers him a month's pay and tells him to get out.

Roger leaves the interview fuming with rage and decides to take Martin to an industrial tribunal for unfair dismissal. Martin kicks himself for not going through the proper procedures and realises that he will now have a battle on his hands.

DISCUSSION POINTS

1. Can you think of any way to make a dismissal interview a positive rather than a negative occasion?

2. 'If the correct disciplinary measures are taken it should not be necessary to dismiss anyone, unless they have committed a very serious offence.' Discuss this statement.

3. Do you think that an employee who is to be dismissed should always be offered the opportunity to leave immediately with payment in lieu of notice?

13
Redundancy Interviews

No one likes making one or more members of their staff redundant. In the economic climate of today, however, there are occasions when this unpleasant task has to be undertaken. You will need to muster all your tact and understanding for a redundancy interview as what you are about to say might prove to be a considerable shock to the person you are interviewing.

There are two main differences between dismissal and redundancy:

1. When a person is **dismissed** they generally deserve such treatment, whereas when a person is made **redundant** they may have done nothing wrong at all.

2. Redundancy relates to the **job**, *ie* it is the job that is redundant, whereas dismissal relates to the **individual**.

DOING THE GROUNDWORK

Ensuring that redundancy is necessary
Redundancy may be necessary for three main reasons:

1. Because that person's job no longer exists, due to reorganisation *etc*.

2. Because of a decline in the volume of business.

3. Because the organisation or company is to close.

If the reason for redundancy is number 2, it may be possible to prevent it happening by taking one of the following steps:

• cutting down on overtime

• not taking on any temps or contract workers so that the

permanent staff can keep their jobs

• putting all the staff on short time working until things pick up.

Informing all staff of impending redundancies

Because rumours can very quickly get out of hand, it is a very good idea to draw up a general policy to use as a guideline before there is any hint of redundancies. If unions are involved this policy can be agreed with them in advance. Items listed might include:

• a list of who should be consulted if redundancy becomes necessary

• a promise to minimise and, if possible, avoid altogether compulsory redundancies

• a promise that the organisation will do all it can to help employees find a new job

• a promise to provide employees with full details of redundancy packages.

Not only should unions agree the general policy but they must also be specifically consulted before any actual redundancies take place. When more than ten employees are to be made redundant both the unions and the Department of Employment need to be notified and specified periods of consultation must elapse before the employees are officially made redundant.

Either the union or you should tell all staff about the impending redundancies, so that they are mentally prepared for what is ahead. You can say that at this stage no firm decisions have been taken on who will be made redundant but that they will be kept fully informed at all times.

Deciding which staff to make redundant

Assuming that redundancy is necessary and that there is a choice to make – *ie* numbers 1 or 2 are the reasons for the redundancy – careful consideration needs to be given over who to choose. Never let your emotions take over here. If, for instance, the job to be axed is done by a single parent, struggling to make ends meet, then do not be tempted to keep that person on and find another job to axe instead. Your loyalty must lie first and foremost with the company or organisation you represent.

Many organisations use the policy 'last in first out' and to many this seems fair, but on the other hand if you have some employees who you know would actually volunteer for redundancy, or who are reaching retirement age anyway, then they may prove to be the best choice.

Checking on their entitlements

Most workers are entitled to receive redundancy pay when they are made redundant. The Employment Protection (Consolidation) Act gives the minimum levels of redundancy pay, but some organisations pay out more to their employees, particularly if they have given many years of valuable service. Check this out carefully in advance, so that you will know what to say when the interview takes place.

Arranging suitable times for interviews

Be tactful when arranging redundancy interviews. Try to hold them at a time when the person will be able to go home straight afterwards to digest the news they have just heard. Of course, if several employees are to be made redundant this might not be possible in which case, if it can be arranged, it would be a nice gesture to offer them the rest of the day off anyway.

CONDUCTING THE INTERVIEW

Showing your regret at the situation

The way you handle a redundancy interview is vitally important. You must show that you are genuinely sorry about the situation that has arisen, but at the same time you need to make it clear that it is not your fault. Tell the employee that you wish you could keep them on, but circumstances are preventing you from doing so. Go on to explain what those circumstances are, outlining exactly why the redundancies are necessary. An explanation will not bring back the employee's job, but it might help them to understand why their job has been singled out.

Of course, your task will be made considerably easier if the person you are interviewing has applied for voluntary redundancy, or is very close to retirement age. In such cases, their only real concern will be the financial package you are going to offer them.

Detailing the financial matters

Once you have got over the first step of explaining why redundancies are necessary, you should then proceed briskly to the financial matters. Give full details of the following:

- the notice period they will be required to work and the date they will be leaving

- the redundancy pay they will be entitled to

- any holiday pay owing

- arrangements to be made for life assurance, pension scheme and any other benefits the employee may have paid in for.

If you bear in mind that an employee's first worry is likely to be financial – 'I've lost my job, how will I afford to live?' – any reassurance you can give them on the financial side will be greatly appreciated.

Being prepared for anger and emotion

However well you handle the interview, your employee may still get very upset and angry over what you are saying to them. This is a natural reaction, particularly if the redundancy is totally unexpected, and you must try to understand their feelings. They will probably say 'Why me?', and if they do, you are going to have to come up with an answer, so think about it in advance.

Offer as much sympathy as necessary. Do not rush the person out as quickly as you can. Talk about their anger and anxieties for the future. Try to impress upon them that they are **not** a failure, and that redundancy does **not** reflect on their ability to do their job well. Guard against being too patronising though. Suggesting that they will walk straight into another similar job because of their undoubted talents would probably be going overboard just a little bit!

Trying to end on a positive note

Once the worst part is over, make an effort to end the interview on a positive note. Tell the employee that you are quite prepared for them to take reasonable time off to go for interviews for other jobs.

Some organisations give employees who are made redundant an **information pack** containing interview hints, a sample CV, application letter *etc*. This can be very helpful and you may like to give it to the employee before they leave the interview room.

If the employee has a company car, you might like to suggest that they can keep it until they get themselves sorted out. There is nothing worse than being made redundant and losing a company car all at the same time.

At the very end of the interview, say to your employee that should you be in a position to employ them again in the future, you will contact them straight away. That, if nothing else, will make them feel that they must have done their job well, otherwise you would not be making such an offer.

FOLLOWING UP

Checking that employees receive their compensation
After the interview has taken place it is up to you to ensure that the employee receives the agreed financial package. Never let anyone leave your employment with less than they should have. Not only will you be breaking your word, but you will also be offering the employee grounds for applying to a tribunal later on.

Arranging references
It goes without saying that whenever a person is made redundant you should always offer them a favourable reference. You could let them prepare it themselves and then agree it, unless it is unreasonable. That way the employee will know what is being said and will presumably be happy with the wording.

Giving encouragement to remaining staff
Redundancies can cause an unsettled workforce. Even though they have been told who is affected, many employees will still fear for their jobs. It may be necessary for you to call a meeting to impress on everyone that their jobs are safe. Say that there are no guarantees in this life, but if everyone works together and creates a successful working team, maximum performance will be achieved and, hopefully, everyone's future will then be assured.

QUESTIONS AND ANSWERS

I've got to make one of my word processing operators redundant. They all work well. How can I possibly decide who to get rid of?
In this situation it would probably be fairest to use the 'last in first out' policy.

I feel really guilty about two redundancies I am being forced to make.

Can I offer these people more than the normal redundancy payments?
Yes, you can. In fact many organisations improve on the minimum
payments required by law.

*I find it very hard to handle emotional females, particularly at
redundancy interviews. What can I do to lighten the situation a little?*
Not a lot, I'm afraid. Redundancy can come as a great shock,
particularly for someone who is absolutely dependent on the money
they earn. After the interview they will probably get things into
perspective and start to think positively again, but whilst the
interview is taking place all you can do is be sympathetic, sincere
and understanding.

CHECKLIST

Before
- Do you have a ready prepared redundancy policy?

- Are you sure that redundancy is the only way out?

- If applicable, have you notified the Department of Employment
  and/or the union?

- Have you spoken to all the staff?

- Have you decided who to make redundant?

- Have you checked on their entitlements?

- Have you thought about when to hold the interviews?

During
- Have you shown how sorry you are about the situation?

- Have you explained why the redundancies are necessary?

- Have you given the employee full details of the financial package
  they will receive?

- Have you successfully dealt with anger and emotion?

- Have you ended the interview on a positive note?

After

- Have you checked that everyone has received their compensation?

- Have you offered references?

- Are you giving ongoing encouragement to the remaining staff?

CASE STUDIES

James gets cold feet

James has been told that he must make one the five customer liaison officers in his department redundant because there is only enough work for four of them. The first thing he does is interview each of them individually to see if they would be willing to take voluntary redundancy. None of them volunteers. He then spends many hours agonising over who to choose, going through each of their backgrounds with a fine-tooth comb to find the person who would be least affected.

Unfortunately for him this turns out to be a middle-aged lady called Jane, who has been with them for five years. She is brilliant at her job but she has a pilot husband and they are certainly not short of money.

James interviews Jane again, who by this time has decided that she does not really mind being made redundant if someone has to go. This makes the interview very easy for him and he congratulates himself on his wise decision. His self-satisfaction is, however, shortlived as he soon comes to realise that Jane was doing as much work as the other four put together.

James gave no thought at all as to how the company would be affected by Jane leaving. At interview, because she almost offered to go he took her up on it willingly. He let his heart rule his head, which proved to be a very unwise move in the circumstances.

Phillip gets it right

The current recession is biting hard into the takings at Phillips's department store and in order to remain competitive he must shed three full-time jobs.

Phillip looks very carefully at all the staff records and chooses three members of staff who are close to retirement age. He interviews each of them in turn and offers them a very attractive redundancy package. He also offers to employ them on an 'as and when' basis in the future, particularly at busy times like Christmas and during staff summer holidays.

Because he is being very fair to them, all three employees accept redundancy willingly. After all, their age would preclude them from working full-time for much longer, but keeping their hand in by filling in on busy occasions suits them all very well.

DISCUSSION POINTS

1. 'Redundancy is a sign of the times.' Discuss what you see as the meaning of this statement.

2. Do you know anyone who has been made redundant? If so, what were their feelings when they were told of the redundancy, and do you think those feelings were justified?

3. Do you think your own attitude is important in a redundancy interview situation?

14
Student Interviews

Students need careful handling, as they are mostly young and inexperienced in both interviews and the ways of the world in general. The wrong treatment can destroy their confidence for ever, and it is very important never to talk to a student in the way a parent would talk to a child. They expect to be treated as responsible adults, and this is the way you should treat them, unless they behave in an irresponsible way.

The kind of students we are dealing with in this chapter are those applying to take a course of training, either at a state college or at a private institution.

DOING THE GROUNDWORK

Reading the paperwork
Students will normally fill in an application form to apply for a place on a training course, so before interviewing them it should be possible to find out some information about their background and any past job experience. If appropriate, it may also be helpful to obtain a school report.

Working out a plan
If a student wishes to take a particular course, you as the interviewer need to assess whether they are going to be able to cope with that course. This means you reading through their application form very carefully and then compiling a list of questions relevant to their particular circumstances. Make sure that your plan for the interview allows some time for the student to voice their thoughts. Although you are the interviewer, they are going to do the course and their questions and worries are as important, if not more important, than your own.

Agreeing an interview time
The golden rule of student interviews is not to arrange too many on

the same day. Although this is true of all interviews, with students you may be helping them to decide their entire future, and this is a big responsibility for you to take on. Interviewing ten students on one day will, almost certainly, ensure that the last four or five end up getting a raw deal because you are tired and therefore unable to give of your best.

However many students are being interviewed, it is important to ensure that the time you choose is sufficient and appropriate. There is nothing more off-putting than being interviewed by someone who looks at their watch every few minutes, because the interview is sandwiched between two other important appointments. Take care to see that, as far as you are aware, you will be able to spend the necessary amount of time with the student when they attend, without continual interruptions.

Before a student interview takes place:

• read the paperwork and gather all the relevant information

• work out your plan, so that you know how long you need to allow for the interview

• check in your diary for a suitable day and time

• write to the student, at least two weeks in advance, advising them of the interview day and time, and asking them to confirm that they are able to attend

• if the student cannot attend at the given time, offer an alternative.

CONDUCTING THE INTERVIEW

Beginning in a reassuring way

As we have said, students need careful handling. Take the time right at the beginning of the interview to put your interviewee at ease. They will probably feel nervous and apprehensive. It may well be their first ever interview, and it is up to you to show that you are not the enemy, that in fact you are only there to help them achieve their aims and ambitions.

Above all, make sure you don't lecture. You may well be a college lecturer as well as an interviewer, but this should not show. Your aim is to hold a friendly conversation where both parties feel able to contribute fully and reach the desired conclusions.

Explaining the set up

Many students apply for courses without having much idea of what they entail. Your job at the interview is to assess their suitability for both the course and the training establishment, and you can only do this if you explain the set up in detail. First of all, talk about what their chosen course would involve. Then, tell them where they would study and if possible take them on a guided tour. This helps them to feel familiar with their surroundings and also gives you a chance to see how you think they would fit in.

Talking about qualifications

Most students take a training course in order to gain the qualifications they need for their chosen career. It is therefore very important for you to explain at the interview exactly what those qualifications are and how they can be achieved. For instance, some examinations are in several parts spread over a number of years and are taken as 'modules', with so many modules equalling the full qualification. Although this might seem a very simple process to you, students may find the various qualifications with their strange initials, such as NVQs, complicated and confusing.

Make absolutely sure that students understand what will be expected of them if they join the training course. **Never understate the work they will have to do**. It is far better to over-emphasise it. At least they will then be prepared for the worst and any improvement in the workload will be a pleasant surprise!

Asking about ambitions

In order to get an overall picture of the students you interview, it is important to ask them about their long-term ambitions. Someone taking a course because their parents want them to, and without any intention of using the qualifications they gain, is not likely to be well motivated and enthusiastic. In a group they might prove to be a 'downer' adversely influencing everyone else. You might well decide that such a person should not be accepted onto a course.

Conversely, an interviewee who enthusiastically tells you about their hopes for the future and their determination to succeed is likely to be an encouraging member of the group, and several positive students working together should achieve positive results at the end of the course.

FOLLOWING UP

Preparing relevant letters and reports

After the interview has taken place you should make notes on what was discussed and agreed upon. If you personally will not be responsible for the training course selected, then you should give a copy of your notes to the person or persons concerned. It may also be necessary to write a letter to the student's current headteacher or employer to confirm the arrangements for training that have been made.

Continuing the assessment

Assuming you have dealt with the interview in a positive way, making relevant notes and coming to a definite decision about the training course the student is to take, there should be no problem with you following through that student as he or she progresses.

Students can, like many of us, choose to take the easy way out and it is very important to ensure that they keep up with their studies and reach the required standard by the required time. This might involve you speaking to various members of staff, or you may be training the person yourself, but either way, continuous assessment is vital.

Carrying out further interviews

It may be necessary to interview the student from time to time to check on progress. This will depend on individual circumstances, but a face-to-face interview occasionally may well be good for the student's morale. They will know that someone is watching over them and, as long as you encourage rather than continually criticise, such interviews should have a very beneficial effect.

QUESTIONS AND ANSWERS

Do I say anything to a student who arrives for interview dressed in leather gear, and with dyed green hair?
Everyone is entitled to their own opinions on dress and hair, within reason, and their appearance need not affect their suitability for the course. After all, someone with dyed green hair may be just as clever as anyone else.

If your training establishment has certain rules about dress, however, you should point these out to the prospective student at interview, so that they can decide whether they are prepared to conform, should they attend for a course. Make sure also that any subsequent tuition on interview technique includes suggestions on proper dress for such occasions.

If I treat a student as an equal, will they still respect me?
Yes, they definitely will, just so long as you let them see that you will only treat them as an equal if they play their part and act accordingly.

Can I interview several students at once, rather than one at a time? This will save me hours in interviewing time.
Students, particularly when they are young, may feel self-conscious, when speaking frankly in front of others. One-to-one interviews are therefore worth the extra time they take up.

CHECKLIST

Before
• Have you read through the relevant paperwork?

• Have you worked out an interview plan?

• Have you agreed an interview time?

• Have you made sure that you have sufficient time and that you will not be interrupted?

During
• Have you begun in a reassuring way?

• Have you explained the details of the college and the course?

• Have you explained what is expected of the students?

• Have you asked about their ambitions?

After
• Have you made notes on what was discussed at the interview?

• Have you sent letters out, if appropriate?

• Have you continued assessing the students?

• Have you arranged follow-up interviews from time to time?

CASE STUDIES

Anna struggles with her interview technique

Anna is new to interviewing having only just been appointed as Head of the Business Studies Department at Longbeach College of Further Education. It is the college's policy to interview all students before they enrol for their courses and this task has fallen on Anna. She arranges the interviews over several weeks, and, although she starts disastrously, she does improve as her confidence grows.

Let us take a look at her first interview. The student, Jane, wishes to take a full-time personal assistant's diploma course. The following is an extract from the proceedings.

Jane enters the room having knocked first. Anna remains seated behind her big, austere desk, and waves Jane to the only available seat in the far corner of the room.

Anna   Hello there, um, (looks down at her notes) Helen is it? No, of course, Jane. Sit down Jane. I'm Mrs Chapman, the Head of Business Studies. I must say I've only just got the job, so I'm not used to interviewing. If I make a mess up you'll have to excuse me. (Anna laughs, looking at Jane briefly and then back at her notes on the desk.) Now, Jane, what did you want to do with us?

Jane   The personal assistant's diploma course, if I can.

Anna   Mmm, now let me look at your qualifications. You didn't do very well with your A-Levels, did you? What went wrong there? Boyfriend trouble was it, or the time of the month? (Ann laughs again at her little joke, while Jane looks at her feet, obviously embarrassed.)

Jane   Actually I had glandular fever at the beginning of the upper sixth and was off for three months. It docs say that on my form, and you will see that the accompanying letter from my headteacher says that he thinks I would have got three Bs under normal circumstances.

Anna   Ah yes, right. Well, you'll probably manage then. Have to work hard though? Can you work hard when you need to, Jane? We don't like failures at Longbeach, you know.

This short passage shows a number of deficiencies in Anna's interviewing techniques:

1. Anna sits behind her desk, whilst Jane sits over the other side of the room, creating a teacher/pupil barrier. It would be far better for the two of them to sit together.

2. Anna introduces herself as 'Mrs Chapman', rather than Anna Chapman, and doesn't manage to get Jane's name right first time.

3. Everything points to the fact that Anna has not properly prepared for this interview. She seems to know nothing at all about Jane's background.

4. To talk about failure to a prospective new student is showing a negative rather than a positive approach, and is likely to upset Jane before she even starts.

Let us now look at a more positive start to the interview:
Anna opens the door to welcome Jane into her room.

Anna   Hello, Jane, do come in and sit down. I'm Anna Chapman, the Head of Business Studies. (Anna shows her to a comfortable chair and then sits herself down beside her.) Now, I understand you would like to take the personal assistant's diploma course. Is that right?

Jane   Yes it is.

Anna   Now, you didn't do too well with your A-Levels, did you, but that was understandable. Glandular fever is really rotten. I had it when I was 19, so I know what you must have gone through. Anyway, your headteacher says you would have got three Bs under normal circumstances, so you must have been working well before your illness. The course does require at least two grade Cs at A-Level if possible. Would you be prepared to take English again, along with the course? Although it is not essential, I think it would be a good idea.

Jane   Yes, I was going to ask if I could do that anyway. I would like to get a good grade, because I think I'm capable of it.

Anna   I'm sure you are Jane, and as long as you are prepared to work hard, you should be able to cope with the course too. Now let me give you some information about the personal assistant's syllabus, so that you will know what is involved ...

This second version shows Anna much more in control of the situation, and whilst she puts the important points across, she still manages to sound human, friendly and interested in Jane and her future.

DISCUSSION POINTS

1. Do you think you should treat students as equals or underlings?

2. How important do you think it is for students to be fully qualified for the course they intend to take?

3. Make a list of the points you think should be discussed at a student interview for a word processing course.

Glossary

Agenda. A programme of items to be discussed at an interview or meeting.

Appraisal. A review of an employee's accomplishments.

Attitude. The way we think or behave, and how we show it.

Behaviour. The way in which people react.

Body language. The way we communicate by using difference parts of our body rather than the spoken word.

Closed questions. Questions requiring a direct and short answer, such as Yes or No.

Communicate. To give, receive or exchange information with others.

Counselling. A type of interview which is held to solve a problem. The interviewer tries to assist the owner of the problem in finding a solution.

Curriculum vitae. (CV), meaning 'the course of a life'; a summary of a person's personal background, education and career.

Delegate. To give a task to another person.

Discrimination. Unfair treatment because of race, colour, sex, religion or other similar factors.

Environment. The surroundings we live and work in.

Evaluate. To review the result of a decision or solution.

Feedback. Information received from other people which may be relevant to the matter in hand.

Health and Safety Act. An Act passed to secure the health, safety and welfare of persons at work.

Induction. An introduction. An induction interview is often held to tell new employees about the organisation they have joined and what their part will be within that organisation.

Interaction. An exchange of thoughts, ideas and proposals.

Interpret. To explain the meaning of something.

Interviewee. A person being interviewed.

Jargon. Specialised language only recognisable to specific groups of people.

Lateral thinking. Creative, rather than logical thinking.

Manager. A person who manages or motivates other people to achieve specific goals.

Media. A term generally used to mean television, radio and the press.

Mentor. Older or more experienced person responsible for guiding a less experienced person.

Monitoring. Keeping a close eye on a situation or problem.

Motivate. To prompt ourselves or others into action.

Objectives. Targets or goals to be achieved.

Open questions. Questions requiring a detailed answer.

Panel. In the context of interviews, a panel is a group of people who conduct an interview between them. A panel is sometimes used for job selection.

Performance. The way in which a person carries out his or her duties.

Rapport. Understanding relationship between people.

Relevant. Applicable to the subject.

Returners. Term used for those people who have, for some reason, taken a break from work and are now returning to the workplace.

Sex Discrimination Act. An Act of Parliament which makes it illegal for employers to discriminate against people on the grounds of their sex or of their marital status.

Skills. Practical expertise needed to do a particular job.

Summary. Résumé of main points made.

Time management. The art of using time effectively.

Under-achieving. Not reaching the required standard.

Waffle. Flowery language which does not come straight to the point.

Further Reading

Conducting Effective Interviews, John Fletcher (Kogan Page, 1995).
Effective Interviewing, Martin John Yate (Thorsons, 1995).
Employment Law, Christopher Waud (Michael O'Mara Books).
How to Communicate at Work, Ann Dobson (How To Books, 1995).
How to Conduct Staff Appraisals, Nigel Hunt (How To Books, 2nd edition 1994).
How to Employ & Manage Staff, Wendy Wyatt (How To Books, 2nd edition 1995).
How to Manage an Office, Ann Dobson (How To Books, 1995).
How to Manage People at Work, John Humphries (How To Books, 2nd edition 1995).
How to Master Public Speaking, Anne Nicholls (How To Books, 3rd edition, 1995).
Interviewing, Glynis M Breakwell (BPS Books, 1990).
Investing in People, Harley Turnbull (How To Books, 1996).
Managing Meetings, Ann Dobson (How To Books, 1996).
Starting to Manage, Julie-Ann Amos (How To Books, 1996).
Successful Interviewing in a Week, Mo Shapiro (Institute of Management, 1993).
Success in Communication, Stuart Sillars (John Murray, 1992).
Taking On Staff, David Greenwood (How To Books, 1996).

Index

HOW TO KNOW YOUR RIGHTS AT WORK
A practical guide to employment law

Robert Spicer

Written in clear English, this easy-to-follow handbook sets out everyone's rights at work whether in an office, shop, factory or other setting. Frequent use is made of recent court cases to illustrate the text. 'Justifiably described as a practical guide to employment law. It is clearly written in language readily understood by the layman... The text has been well laid out and sections are clearly signposted... The extensive use of case study material is interesting and helpful... interesting enough in its own right to be read from cover to cover.' *Careers Officer journal.* 'All in all a welcome addition to the libraries of advice-giving agencies, trade unions and employers alike.' *Frontline.* 'A very useful basic guide.' *Newscheck/Careers Service Bulletin.* Robert Spicer MA(Cantab) is a practising barrister, legal editor and author who specialises in employment law.

141pp illus. 1 85703 009 5.

HOW TO MANAGE YOUR CAREER
Achieving your goals in a changing world

Roger Jones

Would you like a great career, with real job satisfaction, generous pay and conditions? Lots of people already enjoy such careers – and so could you if you manage things in the right way. Should you work for yourself, or perhaps move overseas? In the fast-changing 1990s, developing a successful working life calls for constant attention, learning, and a willingness to adapt. Study the valuable advice in this positive and forward-looking book. Take charge of yourself – and your future. Roger Jones BA MInstAM MIM is a leading author, writer and lecturer on careers topics.

160pp illus. 1 85703 107 5.

SURVIVING REDUNDANCY
How to take charge of yourself and your future

Laurel Alexander

When redundancy hits, you can either view the event as a horror story or as a challenge for positive growth. This book sets out in a helpful way how to survive the first few weeks, both practically and emotionally. It explains how to redefine your work motivations, how to create a professional jobsearch strategy and network your skills, how to approach self employment, contract and temporary work as well as educational and training options. The key to any successful career change is the right psychological attitude, and issues such as dealing with change and positive self talk are explained with case study examples. Laurel Alexander is a manager/trainer in career management who has helped many individuals succeed in changing their career direction.

160pp illus. 1 85703 187 3.

CAREER PLANNING FOR WOMEN
How to make a positive impact on your working life

Laurel Alexander

More women are entering the workplace than ever before. Whether it is on the corporate ladder or self employed, women are establishing a much stronger place for themselves within the world of commerce and industry. As global and national markets shift and business ethos develops, the specific qualities of women play a vital part alongside those of men. Business has been influenced primarily by male thought and action. Now there is the opportunity for women to make a substantial contribution with new ideas and approaches. The book is not about women taking men's jobs or about women being better or worse than men. It is intended to help women understand their unique and emerging role in business, change their perception of themselves and take much more responsibility for their responses and actions within the workplace. Laurel Alexander is a manager/trainer in career development who has helped many individuals succeed in changing their work direction. She is also author of *Surviving Redundancy* in this series.

160pp illus. 1 85703 417 1.

HOW TO APPLY TO AN INDUSTRIAL TRIBUNAL
A practical step-by-step guide for applicants

Robert Naylor

Have you suffered from harassment or discrimination at work? Using actual forms and documents, this book shows you exactly how to apply to an industrial tribunal, how to prepare your case without running up a legal bill, what to do and say at the actual hearing, and even how to appeal – if need be right up to the European Court. 'I particularly liked the way the information is organised with lots of headings, lists of key points, case study material, illustrations and examples... Certainly lives up to its claim of being a step-by-step guide – essential reading.' *Journal of the Institute of Careers Guidance*. Robert Naylor FIPD is Director of Personnel Advisory Services, which since 1985 has helped hundreds of employees succeed in winning claims in Industrial Tribunals all over the country.

140pp illus. 1 85703 042 7.

HOW TO USE THE INTERNET
A practical introduction for every computer user

Graham Jones

The fast-growing Internet is set to revolutionise personal and business communications across the globe, as well as entertainment, information and education. Unlike other books on 'The Net', here is a down to earth practical guide that will help you get the most out of this communication revolution. Gone are the heavy technical introductions, the in-depth computer instructions. Instead, here are simple, straightforward steps that anyone can use to get onto the Net and start exploring the new information super highway. Soon, nearly everyone in the developed world will have access to the Internet. This book shows you how and where to begin. Graham Jones is a leading business consultant and author. He is the author of *How to Manage Computers at Work* in this series, and has contributed to many computer magazines. He is Managing Director of a specialist business that utilises the Internet for up-to-date information.

126pp illus. 1 85703 197 0.

INVESTING IN PEOPLE
How to help your organisation achieve higher standards and a competitive edge

Dr Harley Turnbull

Investors in People is the most important quality programme for change in the 1990s. As Sir Brian Wolfson, Chairman, Investors in People, UK, said (*Employment News*, June 1995), 'Thousands of companies across the country are involved in gaining sustainable, competitive advantage for their business by introducing the winning principles of the Investor in People Standard'. The National Advisors Council for Education and Training Targets has set an Investor in People target for the year 2000: – 70% of all organisations employing 200 or more employees and 35% employing 50 or more, to be recognised as Investors in People. Dr Harley Turnbull, a chartered Occupational Psychologist and Member of the Institute of Personnel and Development, has professional experience of IIP both as an internal HRD manager and external consultant.

192pp illus. 1 85703 188 1.

TAKING ON STAFF
How to recruit the right people into your organisation

David Greenwood

In any organisation three things are sure: people are the key to winning the competitive edge; when a company needs to recruit it's in a hurry; and few things can be as disastrous as a bad recruitment decision. *Taking on Staff* is designed for the manager in a hurry. It is a practical off-the-peg recruitment and selection package suitable for every kind of organisation and job. It covers the whole process from defining the organisation's needs, and ending with the induction of new staff. At every stage it explains how to collect, evaluate and record evidence about a candidate's potential to meet their organisation's needs. The book is complete with checklists, specimen forms, contracts, letters and typical case studies. David Greenwood is Personnel Officer for the Government of the Island of Jersey, and an NVQ Assessor.

160pp illus. 1 85703 189 X.

How To Books

How To Books provide practical help on a large range of topics. They are available through all good bookshops or can be ordered direct from the distributors. Just tick the titles you want and complete the form on the following page.

___ Apply to an Industrial Tribunal (£7.99)
___ Applying for a Job (£7.99)
___ Applying for a United States Visa (£15.99)
___ Be a Freelance Journalist (£8.99)
___ Be a Freelance Secretary (£8.99)
___ Be a Local Councillor (£8.99)
___ Be an Effective School Governor (£9.99)
___ Become a Freelance Sales Agent (£9.99)
___ Become an Au Pair (£8.99)
___ Buy & Run a Shop (£8.99)
___ Buy & Run a Small Hotel (£8.99)
___ Cash from your Computer (£9.99)
___ Career Planning for Women (£8.99)
___ Choosing a Nursing Home (£8.99)
___ Claim State Benefits (£9.99)
___ Communicate at Work (£7.99)
___ Conduct Staff Appraisals (£7.99)
___ Conducting Effective Interviews (£8.99)
___ Copyright & Law for Writers (£8.99)
___ Counsel People at Work (£7.99)
___ Creating a Twist in the Tale (£8.99)
___ Creative Writing (£9.99)
___ Critical Thinking for Students (£8.99)
___ Do Voluntary Work Abroad (£8.99)
___ Do Your Own Advertising (£8.99)
___ Do Your Own PR (£8.99)
___ Doing Business Abroad (£9.99)
___ Emigrate (£9.99)
___ Employ & Manage Staff (£8.99)
___ Find Temporary Work Abroad (£8.99)
___ Finding a Job in Canada (£9.99)
___ Finding a Job in Computers (£8.99)
___ Finding a Job in New Zealand (£9.99)
___ Finding a Job with a Future (£8.99)
___ Finding Work Overseas (£9.99)
___ Freelance DJ-ing (£8.99)
___ Get a Job Abroad (£10.99)
___ Get a Job in America (£9.99)
___ Get a Job in Australia (£9.99)
___ Get a Job in Europe (£9.99)
___ Get a Job in France (£9.99)
___ Get a Job in Germany (£9.99)
___ Get a Job in Hotels and Catering (£8.99)
___ Get a Job in Travel & Tourism (£8.99)
___ Get into Films & TV (£8.99)
___ Get into Radio (£8.99)
___ Get That Job (£6.99)
___ Getting your First Job (£8.99)
___ Going to University (£8.99)
___ Helping your Child to Read (£8.99)
___ Investing in People (£8.99)
___ Invest in Stocks & Shares (£8.99)

___ Keep Business Accounts (£7.99)
___ Know Your Rights at Work (£8.99)
___ Know Your Rights: Teachers (£6.99)
___ Live & Work in America (£9.99)
___ Live & Work in Australia (£12.99)
___ Live & Work in Germany (£9.99)
___ Live & Work in Greece (£9.99)
___ Live & Work in Italy (£8.99)
___ Live & Work in New Zealand (£9.99)
___ Live & Work in Portugal (£9.99)
___ Live & Work in Spain (£7.99)
___ Live & Work in the Gulf (£9.99)
___ Living & Working in Britain (£8.99)
___ Living & Working in China (£9.99)
___ Living & Working in Hong Kong (£10.99)
___ Living & Working in Israel (£10.99)
___ Living & Working in Japan (£8.99)
___ Living & Working in Saudi Arabia (£12.99)
___ Living & Working in the Netherlands (£9.99)
___ Lose Weight & Keep Fit (£6.99)
___ Make a Wedding Speech (£7.99)
___ Making a Complaint (£8.99)
___ Manage a Sales Team (£8.99)
___ Manage an Office (£8.99)
___ Manage Computers at Work (£8.99)
___ Manage People at Work (£8.99)
___ Manage Your Career (£8.99)
___ Managing Budgets & Cash Flows (£9.99)
___ Managing Meetings (£8.99)
___ Managing Your Personal Finances (£8.99)
___ Market Yourself (£8.99)
___ Master Book-Keeping (£8.99)
___ Mastering Business English (£8.99)
___ Master GCSE Accounts (£8.99)
___ Master Languages (£8.99)
___ Master Public Speaking (£8.99)
___ Obtaining Visas & Work Permits (£9.99)
___ Organising Effective Training (£9.99)
___ Pass Exams Without Anxiety (£7.99)
___ Pass That Interview (£6.99)
___ Plan a Wedding (£7.99)
___ Prepare a Business Plan (£8.99)
___ Publish a Book (£9.99)
___ Publish a Newsletter (£9.99)
___ Raise Funds & Sponsorship (£7.99)
___ Rent & Buy Property in France (£9.99)
___ Rent & Buy Property in Italy (£9.99)
___ Retire Abroad (£8.99)
___ Return to Work (£7.99)
___ Run a Local Campaign (£6.99)
___ Run a Voluntary Group (£8.99)
___ Sell Your Business (£9.99)

___ Selling into Japan (£14.99)
___ Setting up Home in Florida (£9.99)
___ Spend a Year Abroad (£8.99)
___ Start a Business from Home (£7.99)
___ Start a New Career (£6.99)
___ Starting to Manage (£8.99)
___ Starting to Write (£8.99)
___ Start Word Processing (£8.99)
___ Start Your Own Business (£8.99)
___ Study Abroad (£8.99)
___ Study & Learn (£7.99)
___ Study & Live in Britain (£7.99)
___ Studying at University (£8.99)
___ Studying for a Degree (£8.99)
___ Successful Grandparenting (£8.99)
___ Successful Mail Order Marketing (£9.99)
___ Successful Single Parenting (£8.99)
___ Survive at College (£4.99)
___ Survive Divorce (£8.99)
___ Surviving Redundancy (£8.99)
___ Take Care of Your Heart (£5.99)
___ Taking in Students (£8.99)
___ Taking on Staff (£8.99)
___ Taking Your A-Levels (£8.99)
___ Teach Abroad (£8.99)
___ Teach Adults (£8.99)
___ Teaching Someone to Drive (£8.99)
___ Travel Round the World (£8.99)
___ Use a Library (£6.99)

___ Use the Internet (£9.99)
___ Winning Consumer Competitions (£8.99)
___ Winning Presentations (£8.99)
___ Work from Home (£8.99)
___ Work in an Office (£7.99)
___ Work in Retail (£8.99)
___ Work with Dogs (£8.99)
___ Working Abroad (£14.99)
___ Working as a Holiday Rep (£9.99)
___ Working in Japan (£10.99)
___ Working in Photography (£8.99)
___ Working in the Gulf (£10.99)
___ Working on Contract Worldwide (£9.99)
___ Working on Cruise Ships (£9.99)
___ Write a CV that Works (£7.99)
___ Write a Press Release (£9.99)
___ Write a Report (£8.99)
___ Write an Assignment (£8.99)
___ Write an Essay (£7.99)
___ Write & Sell Computer Software (£9.99)
___ Write Business Letters (£8.99)
___ Write for Publication (£8.99)
___ Write for Television (£8.99)
___ Write Your Dissertation (£8.99)
___ Writing a Non Fiction Book (£8.99)
___ Writing & Selling a Novel (£8.99)
___ Writing & Selling Short Stories (£8.99)
___ Writing Reviews (£8.99)
___ Your Own Business in Europe (£12.99)

To: Plymbridge Distributors Ltd, Plymbridge House, Estover Road, Plymouth PL6 7PZ. Customer Services Tel: (01752) 202301. Fax: (01752) 202331.

Please send me copies of the titles I have indicated. Please add postage & packing (UK £1, Europe including Eire, £2, World £3 airmail).

☐ I enclose cheque/PO payable to Plymbridge Distributors Ltd for £ _____

☐ Please charge to my ☐ MasterCard, ☐ Visa, ☐ AMEX card.

Account No. ☐☐☐☐☐☐☐☐☐☐☐☐☐☐☐☐

Card Expiry Date ☐ ☐ |9   ☎ **Credit Card orders may be faxed or phoned.**

Customer Name (CAPITALS) ....

Address ....

.... Postcode ....

Telephone .... Signature ....

Every effort will be made to despatch your copy as soon as possible but to avoid possible disappointment please allow up to 21 days for despatch time (42 days if overseas). Prices and availability are subject to change without notice.

BPA